The State in the
Colonial Periphery

The State in the Colonial Periphery

A Study on Sikkim's Relation with Great Britain

R A J I V   R A I

PARTRIDGE

ISBN: Hardcover   978-1-4828-4872-4
                 Softcover   978-1-4828-4873-1
                 eBook   978-1-4828-4871-7

Print information available on the last page.

To order additional copies of this book, contact
Partridge India
000 800 10062 62
orders.india@partridgepublishing.com

www.partridgepublishing.com/india

TABLE OF CONTENTS

Annexures

For
my family

FOREWORD

Borders and bordering regions are getting more attention in the political and strategic thinking in contemporary world as globalization has brought the so called peripheries to the center of debates both on geopolitics and geo-economics. New insights in social sciences that unraveled the colonial impacts which reshaped the very self of the postcolonial societies is also important for anyone engage with the academic endeavors in this regard. This study on Sikkim from the point of view of a colonial periphery looks at some of these issues. As it is mentioned in the book, Sikkim, a small landlocked Himalayan kingdom in South Asia, was never a colony. While stating so, it should also be noted that, the state was fully within the influence of British colonial interest dominant in the region for about two centuries. One can accept the argument that Sikkim was at the periphery of the British colonial interest and it was treated as a peripheral state – colonial periphery - heavily dependent to Great Britain in terms of its political survival. By analyzing the historical developments in the region in general and the relations between Sikkim and Britain in particular since early 19th Century, author contextualizes the background of the developments in Sikkim during mid 20th century.

The book tries to answer certain critical questions which no one has raised in the past such as how do the British influence resulted in the future state formation in Sikkim.

It is obvious that the policies introduced and institutions established by the British in Sikkim ultimately led to decide the destiny of the state even after the end of colonialism in South Asia. The political developments/transformations that had taken place in Sikkim especially during late 1940s and early 1970s points to that direction. As the study concludes, it is the British colonial interests in the region, which became the key factor in determining the political developments and present political situation in Sikkim. The book is useful for any scholar who works on the region or anyone who is interested to know the past and present of Sikkim.

Dr. Sebastian N
Sikkim University, India
May 2015

ACKNOWLEDGEMENTS

When it comes to pay back for the help, support and guidance, which I've received during the course of writing this book, well there's no better way to do it, but by acknowledging their eminent role. But, before I come to the line of courteous people who has played a significant role in making this work worthwhile, there are some great souls, without offering them indebtedness, I would not remain. I shall begin with His Holiness Master Godangel, since people need a reason to live, Master gave me a reason to do something worthwhile, and I owe a great debt of thankfulness to Master. I should thank my teacher, Sir Prem Kumar Subba, who was my Political Science teacher at School, for if he wasn't there, I won't be here today. And lastly, I owe a great debt of indebtedness to Moma (Grandma), whose prayers, love and affection really paid off, thank you for everything you've done for me.

Now I come to the persons whose direct contribution has made this work worthwhile. I shall begin with Dr. Sebastian N. whose critical comments and worthy suggestions has made this work significant and for the inspiration which kept me keep going. I owe a great debt of thankfulness to Dr. Sebastian N.

I am thankful to Shri C. D. Rai and Hon'ble Member of Parliament (MP), Shri P. D. Rai, whose generosity gave me the opportunity to discuss very relevant issues pertaining to my book. Shri C. D. Rai who was, one of the important members of Sikkim State Congress (SSC), formed in 7th December, 1947. I got the first hand information on the things that happened in Sikkim, after the independence of India, incidents connected with its merger etc. At one occasion, Shri C. D. Rai pointed out: "the topic you're dealing with is very interesting, and this will need two or four sittings to discuss fully". I owe a great debt of thankfulness to them.

I owe a debt of gratitude to Dr. Anna Balikci-Denjongpa, Research Coordinator at Namgyal Institute of Tibetology, Sikkim whose concern and the appraisal during the publishing process of the book really helped me to enhance my book a bit. Her numerous contributions in the field of indigenous culture, history and ethnographic films on Sikkim has paved the way for the young scholars like us in Sikkim.

I am very much thankful to Dr. Alex McKay who was generous enough with his time and for the editing of my manuscript to some extend and offering me some valuable comments for the further research in this field with of course the generous help of Dr. Anna Balikci-Denjongpa I am indebted to them.

I owe a great debt of thankfulness to Namgyal Institute of Tibetology, Sikkim particularly Mr. Tenzin Samphel for the reason that, Mr. Samphel provided me with the information and materials which otherwise was impossible. I owe a great deal of thankfulness to him.

I am thankful to Smt. Nalini G. Pradhan, I.A.S, Commissioner-cum-Secretary, Cultural Affairs and Heritage Department, Government of Sikkim, for granting me the access to the relevant documents held at Sikkim State Archives. I am thankful to Mr. L. N. Sharma and staffs, who spent considerable time in searching for the mentioned documents.

I am thankful to HoD, Department of International Relations, Sikkim University, Dr. Manish for providing the best of the idea on the theme which added extra fervour to this work. I am thankful to Dr. Teiborlang and Newton Sir as well, for the reason that they also didn't remain behind in supporting me and providing the best of the knowledge they had on the theme.

I should mention the generosity of our Hon'ble area M.L.A. cum Minister, Shri Arjun Kumar Ghatani for the best wishes and every help that he extended to me and I should not forget the contributions made by Hon'ble Chief Minister, Shri Pawan Kumar Chamling, for making Sikkim what it is today.

Finally, I thank my father and my mother, Mr. D. B. Rai and Mrs. Mani Kala Pradhan along with my brother Rahul and sister Selina, for their support. And, lastly I would like to thank Dr. Satyabrat Sinha, whose insinuation paved the way of the research, I thank them all.

Gangtok, April 2015   Rajiv Rai

CHAPTER I

Introduction

Sikkim as a state, as per the historical records available to us was established in 1642[1] by three Tibetan *Lamas*[2], namely; Lha-tsun Nam-kha Jig-med, Kathog Kuntu bZangpo and mNag-bDag Sem-pa Phun-tsog Ringzing (Namgyal 1908: 15-7) by consecrating Phuntsog Namgyal as the first ruler of Sikkim at Yuk-sam, currently in West Sikkim. The State was ruled by Namgyal Dynasty[3] for 333 years until when Sikkim was merged into Indian Union and became 22nd state of the Indian Union in the year 1975. This book seeks to analyse the patterns, dynamics and dimensions of the relation of

---

[1] The year 1642 corresponds to the Chu-Ta (Water Horse) year of Tibetan calendar on which Namgyal Dynasty was created (Namgyal 1908: 19).

[2] Tibetan Priests

[3] The Dynasty named after the first ruler of Sikkim, Phuntsog Namgyal. Namgyal Dynasty was created in 1642 A. D. by consecrating Phuntsog Namgyal as the first ruler of Sikkim at Yuk-sam. The three Lamas consecrated Phuntsog Namgyal as the first ruler of Sikkim; Lha-tsun Nam-kha Jig-med, Kathog Kuntu bZangpo and mNag-bDag Sem-pa Phun-tsog Ringzing fleeing persecution from Tibet. Twelve generations of the Namgyal Dynasty ruled over Sikkim. The Namgyals trace their descent from Guru Tashi, a Prince of Kham Minyak in eastern Tibet.

1

Sikkim with Great Britain, and its impact on shaping the present day politics in the region. I have focussed on the period, 1817 – 1947, the period when Great Britain had a significant role/influence over the state and politics of Sikkim.

In the early nineteenth Century, Sikkim came into contact with the British East India Company and a treaty was signed between the two. With this, Sikkim became a peripheral state – colonial periphery – of the British East India Company and later British Empire. Here the term "colonial periphery" has been used to describe the relation of Sikkim with Great Britain and the position of Sikkim with regard to British Indian Empire. The significant point here is that Sikkim was never a colony, or a part of the British Empire, though it was heavily under the colonial influence and control, whereas India was a colony and very much part of the British Empire. Therefore, Sikkim's status can be better understood as a "colonial periphery". A full integration with British Colonial Empire would have given Sikkim a "colony" status which had not been the case.

As observed by scholars like A. K. J. Singh (1988), Alastair Lamb (1964) and Alex McKay (2009), British interests in Sikkim was closely related to the British colonial interest in Asia in general, and the Eastern Himalayan region and Central Asia in particular. British interest in Eastern Himalayan states was to create a belt of buffer states, not annexing them under the East India Company, as their interest collided with Russia. The British wanted to protect their interest in Central Asia against Russia. British's entry in the region was in the time of *The Great Game* between British and Russian Empire.

The Formation of Sikkim State:
A Historical Overview

There are many accounts on how Sikkim came into being. Many scholars have the view that, the historical information obtainable about Sikkim is very meagre, and what there was of local record – a very fine manuscript kept at Pemayantshi – was destroyed by the Gorkha irruption in 1814 (Edgar 1969: 17). According to Saul Mullard, 'at present there is a little documentary evidence to indicate the precise origins of the Tibeto-Sikkimese population who ruled Sikkim' (Mullard 2011: 36). It has been said that, the *Rong-Ring* or Lepcha language and the *Rong-Amin* or the Lepcha script survived for many years. The first Rong Panu or Lepcha King, Pohor-tak is believed to have been lived in 320 B. C. (Lepcha 2011/2013: 65). One of the popular perceptions is that, Bhutias[4] destroyed the Lepcha literature, 'containing their traditions and creed and translated their own mythological works into Lepcha language and preached it to the Lepchas as gospels' (Jha 1985: 54). In this regard, Kotturan (1983) observes that before the arrival of the Buddhism, 'the Lepchas had a remarkable literary tradition of their own, the zealous Lamas seem to have destroyed it considering it of pagan origin'. But a lot of it has come down by the oral tradition and has constituted a rich folklore[5].

---

[4] The word 'Bhutia' is of Nepalese origin. Nepali people used to call Lhasa, Bhot. People from Bhot are Bhutias, who settled in Sikkim and ruled Sikkim through Namgyal Dynasty.

[5] In the beginning there was nothing but God – God Rom, so says the Lepcha folklore and he created the world out of earth and rock. He decorated the empty sky with countless stars and he

Similarly, there is a long story of how the name 'Sikkim' came into being. Tibetan people used to call it *Denjong, Demojong and Demoshong. hBras-I Jongs, h Bras-ma-I Jongs and h Bras-gShongs* were also called and the meaning is the same, 'The Valley of Rice' (Sharma 1996: 4). Lepcha[6] people

---

filled the world with plants, animals, and birds. Then he created the Himalayas; the elder brother of all mountains, and many rivers and their tributaries. On the Himalayas there was Kanchenjunga, the snow-clad peak. The God Rom took two handfuls of pure snow from the top of Kanchenjunga. The snow in his right hand then he converted into a man and called him Phadong Thing which meant, "most powerful". And the snow in his left hand he converted into a woman whom he called Najyonguyu which meant "ever fortunate". The Lepcahs believe that these two are the first parents of the Lepcha people. Once the elders of the village of Daramdin met and decided to reach the sky. Accordingly the pot tower rose and rose to a dizzy height, and two men went up with it. Soon it became difficult for those below to see the top or the two men. At dusk the two men thought that they had almost reached the sky and sent down word for a hook to pull the sky down! The men below thought that the two men had already reached the sky and did not need the tower anymore. So they broke it down by just removing the lowest pots. That was the end of the tower and the men on it! (Kotturan 1983: 122-24).

[6] The Lepchas, or as they call themselves, the Rongpa (ravine-folk) claim to be the autochthones of Sikkim proper. Their physical characteristics stamp them as members of the Mongolian race, and certain peculiarities of language and religion render it probable that the tribe is a very ancient colony from Southern Tibet. They know the ways of birds and beasts, and possessing an extensive zoological and botanical nomenclature of their own (Risley 1894/1989: 10). In their manners they much resemble with the Kirants (a tribe which ruled the parts of Nepal before the advent of Prithivi Narayan Shah), but instead of having chosen a Rajpoot chief, they selected for their leader a native of Tibet. The name Rongpa

are considered to be the original inhabitants of Sikkim. They call Sikkim 'Mayal Layang', meaning sacred and invisible land and Lepchas believe that they have been originated in this place and therefore, Sikkim is their motherland. In Tibetan language *Demojong* means 'Happy Country', and in Nepali happy means 'Sukhi', and deriving that 'Sukhi' from *Demojong*, it has been said that the Nepali people gave the name 'Sukhim'. Chopra in *Sikkim (1979/1985*: 1*)* says; 'the present name of the state is of Nepalese origin'. When the British came in India, Sikkim was popularly known as 'Sukhim', and for the British Sukhim became 'Sikhim', and ultimately turned into 'Sikkim', which has no meaning in any of the languages.

After the establishment of Namgyal dynasty in 1642, various monarchs ruled Sikkim. Yuk-sam was the place where the three Lamas consecrated Phuntsog Namgyal as the first ruler of Sikkim (Edgar 1969: 17). However, the event of the consecration has different stories. One popular story, particularly propagated by the Tibetan Lamas is, it was the fulfilment of the prophecy of Guru Rimpoche who visited Tibet in eighth century and prophesied the opening of the hidden land and said; 'the descendents of the then King of Tibet, Khri srong lde btsan would rule Sikkim' (Namgyal 1908: 10, Mullard 2011: 39). However, another account which is acceptable to academics/historians on the establishment of Namgyal Dynasty in Sikkim is, they

---

must be given by the Tibetans, who called the people those who living on the slopes of the mountains. It is said that Nepalese people called them 'Lapchas' after a fish in Nepal noted for its submissive character. The term 'Lapcha' was subsequently modified to pronounce as 'Lepcha' in English (Kotturan 1983: 18)

trace the roots in the religio-political conflict between the Third Dalai Lama and Zhig po gling pa[7] for the pursuit of hegemony in Central Tibet. The Fifth Dalai Lama attempted to refute the teachings of Zhig po gling pa and with the help of Mongol allies he was able to suppress the Dge lugs pa lineage and established himself as the master of Tibet in 1640 (Mullard 2011: 107, Temple 1977: 22, Edgar 1969: 69). This was the reason for the flight of Tibetan Lamas to Sikkim and the formation of the Dge lugs pa state (ibid), for academicians/historians, which later became the Namgyal Dynasty. It is in the reign of Tsugphud Namgyal (1785-1863), the seventh Rajah of Sikkim, for the first time Sikkim came into contact with the British East India Company.

Sikkim and British East India Company: Early Engagements

It is useful to look upon a brief background of Nepalese expansion towards the east of its border and the effects, of this on Sikkim. By 1780s and 1790s Sikkim came under extreme pressure from the eastward expansion of the Gorkha Kingdom[8]. According to Mullard 'most sources claim that

---

[7] Zhig po gling pa was born into the noble family of Snang rtse who were dominant in the Lasha region during the rule of Rin spungs. Zhig po gling pa received religious and political support from the Bri gung pa and the Brug pa and so was also closey allied to the Sde srid of Gtsang. His teachings led to the establishment of Dge lugs pa sect in Tibet (Mullard 2011: 107).

[8] A kingdom of Northern Hindustan, within seventy years its territories were obtained from a great many petty hill states, and kept under by the predominant power of the Gorkhas. The Gorkha kingdom exhibited a form of parallelogram, three sides of which

the first invasion of Sikkim by Gorkhas took place in 1774[9]. However, the actual invasion of the boundaries of Sikkim coincided with the Sino-Nepalese war of 1788-1792' (Mullard 2011: 177). There is a degree of confusion about what actually happened in Sikkim during the war. The Gorkhas did invade Sikkim and captured most of its territories up to the Teesta river including all of the modern districts of South and West Sikkim as well as Darjeeling, which gave Nepal and Bhutan a common border. The Sikkimese Palace Archives contain a number of documents from this period, regarding Sikkimese involvement in the war. For Mullard, "Whilst the role of Sikkimese Generals in the Sino-Nepalese war seems to have been important, in the eventual outcome Sikkim failed to receive the rewards it had hoped for and in fact made considerable losses as a result of the final peace treaty between China and Nepal".

---

were in immediate contact with the British territories, and the fourth, bounded by the Himalayan chain and empire of China. According to the traditions, the Hindus of the mountains (or purbatties) left their own country on its being invaded by the Mohamedan sovereign of Delhi, who wished to marry a daughter of the Chitore Rajah, celebrated for her beauty. A refusal brought destruction on her father and his capital, and to avoid a hated yoke many of the people fled to the hills, about in 14th century. Most of the aboriginal tribes, until the predominance of the Gorkhas, enjoyed their religion and customs unmolested (Hamilton 1828: 302-06). The Gorkha Rajah Prithivi Narayan Shah united all these petty hill states under the Gorkha Kingdom. Since then, it started growing as a dominant power.

[9]   *The East Indian Gazetteer (1828)* says; in A.D. 1788 the Gorkhas invaded Sikkim with an army of about 6,000 men (Hamilton 1828: 548)

However, the unintended result of this was the growing resentment which Sikkim felt towards China/Tibet and Nepal and the desire to reclaim its possessions once and for all (ibid: 177-8).

During the Anglo-Gorkha war of 1814-1816, Sikkim reclaimed its possessions and ignored Chinese demands to avoid any contact with the British. For the British, this war was primarily to open up the trans-Himalayan trade, to open up Tibet for the Indian or British products. As a result of the defeat of the Gorkhas in 1816 and subsequent signing of the Treaty of Titaliya between British and Sikkim (ibid: 178-9) in 1817, the lost territories of Sikkim during the Gorkhas invasion in 1788-1791 (Mullard 2010: 140) and also during the Sino-Nepalese war of 1788-1792, were regained (Mullard 2011: 179). The rumour of the Gorkhas and Bhutanese intriguing together against the British made the opening of the relations, 'a political and military necessity for the British' (Jha 1985: 2).

Even though, the Treaty of Titaliya did not provide justice to Sikkim in full manner as most of its territories were left with Nepal and even the areas in and around Titaliya was not handed over to Sikkim, rather East India Company kept it in their own possession (Sharma 1996: 51). Company did so because these areas are closer to the border of Nepal and these are plain areas. The company considered Sikkim as its ally against the common enemy, Nepal (Rao 1972: 177) and from these areas British India checked the Nepalese interest of the expansion of the territories.

In the treaty, it was decided that East India Company would transfer in its full sovereignty the hilly or mountainous region situated to the eastward of the Mechi River and to the westward of the Teesta River, formerly occupied by Nepal, and later surrendered to the East India Company, by the treaty signed at Sugauli in 1815[10] to Rajah of Sikkim and his successors. It was also decided that the Sikkimpati Rajah and his successors should abstain from any acts of aggression or hostility against the Gorkhas settled in the region between east of Mechi river and west to Teesta river during the expansion of Gorkha Empire in 1780s till 1815, or any other states. It is also decided in the agreement that, if any disputes or questions that arise between subjects of Sikkim (Gorkhas or any other) and Nepal, or any other neighbouring states, all such issues of conflict should be referred to the adjudication of the East India Company and to abide by the decision of the Company[11].

It is observed by P. R. Rao that the 'Treaty of Titaliya marked the beginning of the end of Sikkim's existence as an independent state' (Rao 1972: 30). By this Treaty the Company gained many political and commercial privileges from Sikkim. The annexation of Darjeeling was the result of that which took place shortly after the signing of the treaty, in 1835. It was an event of great importance in the history of British relations with Sikkim. It not only placed the British into close contact with the hill states of Nepal, Bhutan and Sikkim, but also provided a constant reminder of the possibilities of trade with Tibet (ibid: 177-8), which Tibetans were avoiding since the time of Warren Hastings in the later half of the eighteenth century (Younghusband 1910/1994/2002: 5).

---

[10] See Annexure: I

[11] See Annexure: II

End of British East India Company and its Implications on Sikkim

In 1857, Great Britain had to bring the British East India Company to an end as a result of the bloody conflict often described by some historians as the "first war of independence" (Meyer 2005: 15). However, the British officials in India were in a long run to expand the British territories at any cost, which British government could not afford due to the international obligation and Great Britain's war with other states. The annexation of Darjeeling is an example how an official monopolised power and appealed British government to approve the integration of Darjeeling hills to the British East India Company, later government approved it, and subsequently Darjeeling was granted a subservient position under Bengal Government, in 1835. Another instance is Younghusband's intention to bring Tibet into the direct rule of British government which British Government never approved because Government of Great Britain thought, as much it grows bigger it will become more vulnerable. The over power play of the British officials is another reason for the end of British East India Company.

Even though the 1857 uprising was ultimately crushed by the British, it forced Britain to reassess its governance in South Asia. Control over its vast Indian possessions and civil and military services were transferred in 1858 from the East India Company to the Crown. British followed the policy of acquiring the allegiance of Maharajahs, of what they termed as princely states, allowing them to retain a degree of autonomy while holding protectorate status and cooperating with the Company in trade and natural resources (ibid:

15). In case of Sikkim, Sikkim was never a princely state of British India[12]. Rather the treaty signed between Sikkim and British in 1817 made Sikkim Company's ally and later the treaty signed between British India and Sikkim in 1861 made Sikkim a protectorate state which is inherited by India after 1947.

The Importance of Sikkim in the Power Politics in the Eastern Himalayan Region

The intrigues for control of Central Asia played out between Great Britain and Russia at the end of nineteenth century, which came to be known as *The Great Game.* The British, particularly the cadre[13] in India, were obsessed with the fear that the Tsar's armies would penetrate in the South and threaten British India across from the Himalayas. Both sides sent their spies into the vast and unfamiliar lands of Central Asia, in search of information on the other's movements and intentions. Throughout the nineteenth century, the Tsarist armies had been on the move, ruthlessly extending the Russian Empire. After repulsing Napoleon from Moscow in 1812, the Tsar launched an aggressive expansionist campaign into the Central Asia. In a systematic drive to the east in 1825, his hard-steppes Cossack warriors occupied all the lands between the Caspian Sea and the Aral Sea. It was said that the fearless horsemen formed a veritable moving

---

[12] Sikkim had never appeared in the debates on integration of Princely States. If Sikkim were treated as a princely state of India then it would have been also appeared in the efforts made to merge into Indian Union, which did not happen.

[13] British officials in India.

fence on the borders of Russia, which they extended at a breathtaking rate throughout the nineteenth century. They conquered additional territory from 1846 until 1873, when they reached the northern border of Afghanistan. From 1880 to 1895 they pushed into Central Asia, reaching the Silk Road crossroads of Kashgar in western China, where they created a consulate and established a political presence and a valuable listening post (ibid: 17)

The four small Eastern Himalayan Kingdoms – Tibet, Sikkim, Bhutan, and Nepal – had their own geo-strategic significance in keeping Great powers aloof from coming into direct contact. Located between two great western rivals (England and Russia), was a little-explored country of Tibet, which was viewed by the British forward group[14] as strategically critical in guarding the northern frontier from the Russian infiltration and control. In reality Tibetan geopolitics also involved another key player in the region, China. The struggle between China and Tibet for dominance of Central Asia had been going on for centuries, and at times Tibet occupied vast areas of western China, and at other periods the Chinese controlled much of the Tibet. By the end of the nineteenth century, the Chinese claimed suzerainty over Tibet which was later recognised by the British government. In confirmation to this, the Tibetan Government accepted the presence of a Chinese representative, called the Amban[15] at Lhasa (ibid: 17-8).

---

[14] Supporter of Imperial expansion at any cost – the "forward school" of thought – the advocate of an aggressive imperialistic foreign policy (Meyer 2005: 16).

[15] Amban, an agent of China who residing in Tibet's capital of Lhasa, represented Chinese interests in Tibet and advised the Tibetan government on political issues (Meyer 2005: 18)

The British had recognised Chinese suzerainty over Tibet, so by the end of the nineteenth century when the diplomatic discussions were held between British and China to define borders between Tibet and Sikkim, both the parties were not included in the Convention of 1890[16] (ibid: 18). Tibet and Sikkim were not included in the convention because Tibet was under the suzerainty of China and synonymously Sikkim was under the protection of British India. The two super powers thought whatever policies they impose upon Sikkim and Tibet, will have to be accepted. But the Tibetans refused to recognise the agreement and instead claimed absolute independence from China (ibid: 86-9) but Sikkim did not do that and accepted all the clauses imposed by the colonial master. Meyer (2005: 86) calls it a terminal fault.

According to Meyer (2005), "the small mountain kingdom of Sikkim had the economic blessing and military misfortune to be located on the two most accessible natural routes between Tibet and India. The first route starts from Gyantse in Southern Tibet, across Tibet's Chumbi Valley, Sikkim's Jelep La to the Nathan Valley, and onward to India. The second route began in Shigatse and continued south through Sikkim, and onward to the tea centre of Darjeeling and finally to Calcutta, the official heart of British India" (ibid: 19).

---

[16] Chinese felt that unless they come to an agreement with the British, their influence in Tibet would be threatened. The Government of India was not very anxious to open the negotiations, unless the Chinese were prepared to accept its exclusive supremacy in Sikkim. In 1890 Convention China recognized Sikkim as protectorate state of British India and did not interfere in the affairs of British especially its relation with Sikkim.

Though these two routes were critical for the trade of salt and tea, they also posed a threat to the British because they offered potential passage for northern soldiers to pour into Sikkim, essentially slipping through India's back door. In this way Sikkim was a key strategic outpost in the Great Game where a firm British presence was deemed essential. The Maharajahs' loyalty to Tibet, and to China as the suzerain who wielded protective power over Sikkim, was a long-rooted historic fact. The Maharajahs' annual payment of symbolic token gifts to the Chinese emperor was the further evidence of the subservient relationship to China.

The Sikkim Palace Archives contain lots of letters exchanged between Sikkim and Chinese Amban, in this regard. In the late 1800s, the British had to assume that in the case of conflict, the Maharajah of Sikkim would be a potential friend and ally of the Tibetans (ibid: 20), because firstly, geographically and culturally Sikkim draws closer proximity to Tibet and secondly, the ruling class of Sikkim were Bhutia of Tibetan origin. The Maharajahs of Sikkim had, for centuries, married Tibetan aristocratic women and thus maintained strong family ties with Tibetan power structure. Historically, Sikkim had been threatened and at times partially occupied by the outside forces such as Bhutanese and the Nepalese armies. In such occasions, the Maharajah often fled to Tibet, in Chumbi Valley – considered as a diplomatic enclave – of Lhasa where Maharajah was given refuge by Dalai Lama (ibid: 19-20).

The British were infuriated when the Tibetans constructed a fort at Lingtu in the Nathang Valley in 1886, 12 miles inside the Sikkimese border (ibid: 20). H.

M. Durand, then Secretary to the Government of India, summed up the situation as;

> "There remains the unpleasant fact that the Tibetans are holding a piece of Sikkim. Tibet and China do undoubtedly exercise a certain influence in Bhutan, Sikkim and Nepal, but we do not want that influence increased and solidified. Sikkim stands in a very peculiar position. It is by treaty practically an Indian feudatory state[17]... Nevertheless, Maharajah is much in the hands of the Tibetans. It will, I fear, be difficult to get them out of the country if they take a fancy of staying there and assert claims to suzerainty. Any discussion on these points with China might have very embarrassing results" (Rao 1972: 82).

As it indicates, the Provincial Administration of Bengal was very much worried of the continued Tibetan presence in Sikkim as it resulted in a severe damage to the prestige of British in Eastern Himalayan states. The Lieutenant-Governor of Bengal wanted the Government of India to take steps to ensure the immediate withdrawal of the Tibetans from Lingtu. For securing this object, he made three alternative suggestions; negotiations with the Tibetan frontier officials, intervention of China and, the use of force. As to the first suggestion, he felt that negotiations with local officers were

---

[17] Sikkim was not a feudatory state in its precise meaning, as it was understood in the British India. Sikkim was neither independent nor outside the zone of British interest, during the British period.

of no use. The second proposal that China's intervention was mentioned casually and not discussed fully. He felt that as a final resort, force had to be used. The Tibetans showed their intention to annex Lingtu permanently by consecrating the spot. The Bengal Government asked the Government of India to use force to expel the Tibetans, either by the Deputy Commissioner of Darjeeling or by the Sikkim *Dewan* (Chief Minister) supported by the British arms (ibid: 89).

The Government of India rejected the suggestion as it feared that any forceful expulsion of the Tibetans from Lingtu might be viewed by the Chinese as an attempt to force a passage into Tibet and it might result in all stoppage of the trade on the Sikkim - Tibet frontier. In view of these considerations, the Government of Bengal to much was allowed to warn Maharajah of Sikkim of the probable consequences of his practical abandonment of Sikkim (ibid: 84-6). That time the Maharajah[18] of Sikkim had taken refuge in Tibet's Chumbi Valley due to the probable intervention of the British army. Government of Bengal made several invitations to Maharajah to visit Darjeeling, but Maharajah declined the invitations and informed the Government of Bengal, that he was bound to China and Tibet by the Treaty signed in 1886, the – Treaty of Galing – and he is not allowed to enter into the British territories (ibid: 86).

Risley in *The Gazetteer of Sikkim (1894)* says, 'the treaty of Galing is peculiar in the history of Sikkim. In 1880, one of the Tibetan Secretaries of State accompanied by a Chinese military officer went to Paro in Bhutan for settling some

---

[18] Title of Maharajah accorded to the ruler of Sikkim in 1861 through the Treaty of Tumlong.

local disturbances. On their return to Phari, in Tibet, an unsuccessful attempt was made to extract a similar agreement from Sikkim. Six years later, the subject was reopened, and a formal treaty was signed at Galing, in Tibet, by the Rajah, on behalf of the people of Sikhim, priests and laymen', the treaty read as follows:

> "From the time of Chogel Penchoo Namguay (first Rajah of Sikhim) all our Rajahs and other subjects have obeyed the orders of China. You have ordered us by strategy or force to stop the passage of the Rishi river between Sikhim and British territory; but we are small and the sarkar (British Government) is great, and we may not succeed, and may then fall into the mouth of the tiger-lion. In such a crisis, if you, as our old friends, can make some arrangements, even then in good and evil we will not leave 'the shelter of the feet of China and Tibet. . . . We all, king and subjects, priests and laymen honestly promise to prevent persons from crossing the boundary" (Risley 1894/1989: VIII).

Government of India waited for the right time to intervene, the inaction of the government was criticised both in India and England. Dufferin, then Governor General, finally decided to expel Tibetans from Lingtu by force (Rao 1972: 90). The Tibetans justified their actions as on their own border. To protect the British interests in the region, the British military forces entered Sikkim in 1888, destroyed the Lingtu fort and occupied the capital city of Gangtok and the residence of Maharajah (Meyer 2005: 20). A justification of the British position was later laid out in the *Gazetteer of Sikkim (1894),* "that the obligation of driving the Tibetans out of Sikkim was imposed on us by the essential conditions of our policy towards the East Himalayan states, and that this policy is just and reasonable" (Risley 1894/1989: VXI-VXII).

The following year a British Officer, John Claude White, was called upon as the first British Resident in Sikkim. After receiving the news of the secret treaty of 1886 and Amban's disagreement to change the official relations between Tibet and Sikkim, it was decided to arrange the administration of Sikkim according to the need of the British. White was accordingly appointed as the Political Officer of Sikkim to look after and rearrange the administration of Sikkim (Jha 1985: 29) and to oversee the building of infrastructure, namely roads and bridges that would support the movement of the Indian army into the area, if necessary (Meyer 2005: 20). The Governor of Bengal had been entrusted to administer the British interests in Sikkim, on behalf of the Viceroy, but by 1889 the British could not ignore a growing awareness that the trade routes through these mountains offered a potential military access to India from the north (ibid: 50), that's why they posted Political Officer in Sikkim and who was entrusted to look upon the affairs of Bhutan and Tibet also.

White was posted to Sikkim just one year before the Governments of India and China settled Sikkim's status in the Anglo-Chinese Convention of 1890, which has been briefly discussed earlier. Tibetans refused to recognise the agreement but Sikkim had not enough power to do that.

In the Convention it was decided that, 'the Teesta river watershed would be the border between Tibet and Sikkim. The watershed flowing north would be Tibetan territory while that flowing south would be Sikkim'. Under the terms of the Convention, the Indian Government obtained the right to make administrative decisions regarding Sikkim's internal affairs, frontiers and foreign relations, essentially absorbing Sikkim into the British India (ibid: 50-2).

As a British protectorate, Sikkim enjoyed a special status, compared to other princely states. With this agreement, the Raj obtained effective control over the gateway from Tibet into India via Sikkim, whose importance had been demonstrated by the 1888 Lingtu affair. Moreover, White encountered the Tibetan aggression first-hand while surveying on the northern border in 1890. Inside the Sikkimese territory, some 15 miles south of Tibet in the Langpo Valley, he had encountered Tibetan soldiers who demanded that he immediately get out of 'their' territory (ibid: 52).

The Governor of Bengal established a Council to govern Sikkim, comprised of White as Chairman[19] (ibid). Thus White found himself unexpectedly inserted in the middle of the political and diplomatic melange. Although White's appointment was made for political and military reasons, it also had a substantial effect on Sikkim's socio-economic and internal political situation. 'Maharajah Thutob Namgyal,

---

[19] The Rajah, the Phodang Lama and Dorje Lopen to represent the Lamas, the Khangsa Dewan, Purboo Dewan, Gangtok Kazi, Tashiding Kazi to represent the lay interest, Shew Dingpon as the writer. The Council's function was to collect revenue, listen to appeals and to manage the ordinary affairs of the state (Jha 1985: 33).

together with his Bhutia aristocracy, owned all of the land, while Lepchas, the original inhabitants of Sikkim, were forest-dwellers living in the middle hills as hunters and gatherers' (ibid). Alex McKay adds to it, "many of the Lepchas were also land-owners and there were many mixed clans of Lepcha-Bhutia, the British – divide-and-rule – principle governs their understanding of local identities". Sinha (2008) says 'the – blood brotherhood – between the Bhutia rulers and the Lepchas led to the emergence of a new social class of Kazis in Sikkim', who owned maximum lands. White created the necessary legal and administrative structure for transforming the land relations in Sikkim (Meyer 2005: 52).

White surveyed the lands, divided them into parcels and was instrumental in offering them to the leading Gorkhali families to manage under a well-codified land tenure system. Gorkhalis developed agriculture on large scale, primarily rice and cardamom, by using the techniques of terrace farming. The forest areas were scheduled to be protected and private cultivation tracts were legally described. The land-use changes under White were the beginnings of the gradual decline of the absolute power of the Maharajahs and Kazi aristocracy (ibid).

White suggested the Government of India that Sidkeong Namgyal, the second son of Maharajah to be brought to Darjeeling for the education, so that, in case of need, he could better serve the British interests. The Maharajah's second son, Sidkeong Namgyal, was brought to Darjeeling and arrangements were made for his education. Maharajah objected to the education of his son in English on the ground that the prince was an incarnation of Phodung

Lama[20], but the Bengal Government informed him that the arrangements would be reconsidered if his eldest son was brought to Darjeeling. By making arrangements for the education of Sidkeong Namgyal, Sir Charles Elliott, then Governor of Bengal wanted to put pressure on the Maharajah to bring back his eldest son from Tibet who was receiving education in Tibet (Rao 1972: 112).

The Government of Bengal was very anxious that the Maharajah's eldest son Tchoda Namgyal should not prolong his stay in Tibet, since the British relations with that state were not good. Therefore after making arrangements for the education of Sidkeong Namgyal, the Government of Bengal sent Nolan, Commissioner of the Rajshahi Division, to interview the Maharajah and persuade him to bring back his eldest son from Tibet. The Maharajah once again declined to bring back his eldest son from Tibet on the pretext that it would interfere with his education (ibid: 112). The fact that Maharajah was not willing to bring back his elder son, it was told by the Shew Dewan[21] that 'as soon as the Kumar[22] comes down, he himself would be set aside and the Kumar would be proclaimed as Rajah and His Highness would be deposed or pensioned off on a small allowance' (Namgyal 1908: 113). After this interview with the Maharajah, Nolan suggested the Government of India that the Maharajah should be 'temporarily' deposed and kept under the house arrest. Sir Charles Elliott supported the proposal of Nolan as he felt that by temporarily deposing the Maharajah, the

---

[20] A Head Lama and the founder of Phodung Monastery in North Sikkim.

[21] One of the Ministers of Maharajah Thotub Namgyal.

[22] Eldest son of Maharajah Thotub Namgyal, Tchoda Namgyal.

Government of India could exert pressure on him to get back his eldest son from Tibet (ibid: 112).

Sir Charles Elliott felt that the Maharajah's eldest son, Tchoda Namgyal 'should not be exposed to anti-British influences in Tibet during his formative period'. Moreover, he was anxious for the return of Tchoda Namgyal since the succession of the Maharajah's second son, Sidkeong Namgyal, was riddled with inherent difficulties as he was considered, by the people of Sikkim, to be the Avtar or incarnation of the founder of the Phodung monastery and as such ineligible for temporal duties (ibid).

Sir Charles Elliott was conscious about the public announcement of the Maharajah's temporary deposition might create an uproar in the press. He, however, felt that the formal announcement of the Maharajah's temporary deposition may be good in three ways: first it would prevent the Dewan and the Kazis of Sikkim from obeying the Maharajah's orders, if he were to incite them to defy the British authority. Second, it might bring about some improvement in the Maharajah's own sentiments and lead him to obey the orders of the Government of India. Third, the Maharajah's eldest son Tchoda Namgyal who was believed to be under the control of his relations in Tibet might make an effort on his own part to accept the summons of the Government of India, and come to Darjeeling and he might forfeit his right of succession (ibid: 113).

In view of all these advantages, Sir Charles Elliott, advised the Government of India to disregard any possible outcry and inform the Maharajah that he was deposed for a period of three years and the affairs of his Kingdom would be managed by the British Political Officer and the Council as it was done before during his absence. The Lieutenant-Governor of Bengal felt that at the end of three years, the Government of India could decide whether to restore the throne to the Maharajah or to install his second son in his place. He felt that no practical advantage was likely to be gained by withholding the announcement of the Maharajah's temporary deposition and by merely retaining him under surveillance (ibid).

The Government of India accepted the recommendation of Sir Elliott and deposed the Maharajah, for three years, beginning from July 1892. The British Government however withheld the formal announcement of the deposition of Maharajah as it might provoke excitement or attract attention. After the temporary deposition of Maharajah Thotub Namgyal, the pro-British Sikkim Council addressed a letter to the Maharajah's eldest son Tchoda Namgyal making it clear to him 'that it would be to his advantage to return to Sikkim and he might imperil his right of succession to the throne'. The young prince, in reply, informed the Council that he could not return until his education was completed or without the orders of the Maharajah. On receiving the above reply, the Sikkim Council, which was under the influence of White, recommended the Government of India that the Maharajah's second son, Sidkeong Namgyal should succeed his father. The Council, through one of its important members, the Phodung Lama, explained to the Commissioner of Darjeeling that Sidkeong Namgyal's position as an Avtar Lama would not prevent him from marrying or from ruling the Sikkim kingdom, since he had not taken the final vows. The Phodung Lama further explained to the Commissioner that no religious dispensation from Tibet was necessary to release the young prince from his Avtarship. The Commissioner in reply informed Phodung Lama that time had not come to think about a permanent arrangement since the Maharajah might obey the Government of India's orders and/or the eldest son might return to Sikkim from Tibet (ibid: 113-4).

In early 1895, Thotub Namgyal informed Government of India that he was prepared to obey Government's orders and requested that he may be restored to the throne. In April 1895, Sir Charles Elliott visited Gangtok and informed the Sikkim Council about Maharajah's decision. The Council opposed the restoration of Thotub Namgyal and expressed their wish that he should be permanently deposed and his second son Sidkeong Namgyal should be made the Maharajah. This was expected as the personal relations between the Maharajah and Claude White, the Chairman of the Council, was not good. Sir Charles Elliott proposed to the Government of India that Maharajah Thotub Namgyal might be restored to his position on the following conditions, namely; that he should write to his elder son, Tchoda Namgyal and bring him back from Tibet to Sikkim, and he should accept the new Constitution provided for his Kingdom[23]. The Maharajah accepted the conditions lay

---

[23]   Under the new Constitution, the administration of Sikkim was to be controlled by the Council of leading monks and laymen presided over by the Maharajah when present and, in his absence, all decisions were to be submitted to him. If the Maharajah differed on any point with the Council, the matter was to be referred to the Political Officer and if he agreed with the Maharajah, the Council was bound to yield. The decision of the Council was to be carried out in the joint names of the Maharajah and the body (Rao 1972: 115).

down by the Government of India and in November 1895, Maharajah was restored to his throne (ibid: 114-5).

As regard to the successor to the Sikkim throne, Sir Charles Elliott did not seem to be in consonant with the view of White that all classes of the Sikkim population would welcome the succession of the Maharajah's second son Sidkeong Namgyal. He felt that the objections of different monasteries to the succession of an Avtari Lama could not be easily removed. He, however, advised the Government of India to make proper arrangements for the education of Sidkeong Namgyal, as a possible successor to Sikkim's throne. The Government of India accepted the advice of the Lieutenant-Governor of Bengal and placed Sidkeong Namgyal under the tutelage of Sarat Chandra Das at Darjeeling. He was taught English, Hindi as well as Tibetan (ibid: 115).

Through his well calculated moves and policies, White made Sikkim a well integrated and peaceful corner of British India (Meyer 2005: 54). As a matter of fact, British India never extended its direct control over Sikkim or on any of the Eastern Himalayan states, except some interims. British kept this region as an integrated zone of influence because of the fear that Russia would penetrate into India from Central Asia and through Eastern Himalayan region. The British kept these states as its "colonial peripheries". These states were in a way dependent to Great Britain in terms of political, military and economic survival as the way peripheries are dependent to the core countries. To put it in other words, these states were made to be dependent on British India through various treaties, covenants, and agreements. The remarks of Charles

Bell[24] prove this intention of the British government to make these states dependent on British India. On such account, Bell states that; 'make the Tibetans economically and militarily dependent on us to just that extent that is desirable' (McKay 2009: 66). According to Alex McKay, Bell clearly states on the several occasions that he sought to make the Tibetans dependent upon the British. It was not only with Tibet but true with other peripheral states, which were on the Himalayan borders of British India.

The British relation with Eastern Himalayan states was structurally different from India as the latter was a colony of the British whereas four of the Eastern Himalayan states and Afghanistan in Central Asia, were never under direct colonialism, though they are heavily shaped/influenced by the colonialism during nineteenth and twentieth century. What changes this influence brought upon these states is a concern to ponder upon[25].

Survey of Literature

The literatures have been reviewed in order to identify the knowledge gap on the theme under discussion ranging from the state formation, history of Sikkim to the subsequent developments. An important work reviewed is Saul

---

[24] Political Officer of Sikkim after Claude White.

[25] But, when this question was put forward to Mr. P. D. Rai, Honourable Member of Parliament (MP) about Sikkim being under the indirect colonialism of Britain, since the time when British came into contact with Sikkim. He totally disregarded this argument and said Sikkim was under direct colonialism because everything was controlled by the Political Officer at Gangtok.

Mullard's *Opening the Hidden Land: State Formation and the Construction of Sikkimese History (2011)*, where he says, it was in the period of the British expansion in the Sikkimese Himalayas that a number of Sikkimese histories were written. He has identified three important sources written in this period and has drawn much in his study from these sources. First and latest, the *'Bras ljongs rgyal rabs (BGR)*, which was written in 1908, attributed to Maharajah Thotub Namgyal and Maharani Yeshe Dolma, another is *The Gazetteer of Sikkim (GoS)* written in 1894, and the last one and the earliest, *Bla ma che mtshan gsum 'bras ljongs sbas gnas phebs tshul (BMS)*, written in 1860. He has compared these sources and has come out with an appropriate answer that which source would be more appropriate source for the study. Except *The Gazetteer of Sikkim (1894)*, the other two sources are written in Tibetan language, the earliest history of Sikkim recorded is in Tibetan language, the historians translated it into English.

Another is the *Royal Records: A Catalogue of the Sikkimese Palace Archives (2010)* complied by Saul Mullard and Hissey Wongchuk. This study is the compilation of various treaties, agreements, petitions, personal letters, receipts and other miscellaneous documents exchanged between the Durbar of Sikkim and the British and with others, at the time of British expansion in the Eastern Himalaya.

Alastair Lamb's *The China-India Border: The Origins of the Disputed Boundaries (1964)*, is an important work where he has discussed the belief that Sino-Indian relations over the common border could be conducted with mutual respect for each other's territorial integrity and sovereignty. He has discussed in brief "The Great Game" of nineteenth century and has said now non-imperialist powers are playing the Great Game.

P. R. Rao's *India and Sikkim: 1814-1970 (1972),* he has discussed the relations between the British India and Sikkim in detail right from the beginning of the relation till the end of British rule in India. He has also discussed the transformations which Sikkim witnessed till 1970 as an Indian protectorate. His sources are mainly the documents of the India Office Records and British Library in London.

Another important work is the *History of Sikkim: Unpublished Typescript attributed to Chogyal and Gyalmo (1908),* this piece of work is written by the then Maharajah and Maharani of Sikkim, where they have incorporated the elements of mysticism also; stories about how the Namgyal Dynasty in Sikkim was established, the prophecy of Guru Padmasambabha etc. They have incorporated all the elements best known to them till their time. This piece of work was in Tibetan language in its original form, a former British Political Agent had the history translated by the well known Lama and the author, Dawa Kazi Samdup (Rock 1953: 925).

A. K. J. Singh's *Himalayan Triangle: A Historical Survey of British India's Relations with Tibet, Sikkim and Bhutan 1765-1950 (1988),* derived major part of it from the India Office Library and Records. He has given a comprehensive account of British relations with Tibet, Sikkim and Bhutan. The book discusses the British policies towards the Eastern Himalayan states, and he has discussed of the Great Game going on between Tsarist Russians and the British and the implications of this Game on the Eastern Himalayan states.

Alex McKay's *Tibet and the British Raj: The Frontier Cadre 1904-47 (2009),* explain the developments since Sikkim was the suzerain of Tibet, the British relations with Sikkim affected the Sikkim's relations with Tibet. Alex McKay has analysed the Tibet relations with British India from the perspective of British officials which he says, the Tibetan frontier cadres. After the opening of the British relations with Tibet in 1904, subsequently cadres developed cordial relations with Tibetan people. In an advice to the Tibetan Government, Charles Bell a frontier cadre according to Alex McKay said; 'Britain is giving more power to India, who will hardly show the same friendship... or have the same power to help Tibet'. Tibetan frontier cadres were sympathised to the Tibetans, and it was the officers, Richardson, Gould and Ford of the British GoI (Government of India) who were instrumental in the creation of the Tibet Society of UK, in 1959.

B. S. Das's *The Sikkim Saga (1983),* gives an account of the series of events that took place after his appointment as the Prime Minister of Sikkim following the turmoil that led to the collapse of the administration in Sikkim. He allegedly says the merger of Sikkim took place due to the ambitions of three ladies, namely; Hope Cook who wanted to become the Maharani of the independent Sikkim, Elisa Maria[26], who wanted to become first lady of the state, and Mrs. Indira Gandhi's realpolitik changed the status of Sikkim from protectorate to a state.

B. S. K. Grover's *Sikkim and India: Storm and Consolidation (1974),* analyses the status of Sikkim under British rule and the status of Sikkim vis-à-vis independent

---

[26] Wife of L. D. Kazi, the first Chief Minister of Sikkim.

India. He says, 'Dynamic and ideologically consistent policies have been followed by Smt. Indira Gandhi and these have been firmly executed by the officials of the Ministry of External Affairs'. He says Sikkim, a religious place, turned into an army base.

George Kotturan's *The Himalyan Gateway: History and Culture of Sikkim (1983),* where he discusses the initial question of state formation, the relations of Sikkim with British India and independent India. He says before the advent of the British in the region, India did not bother about the states in the peripheries.

In his book *History of Sikkim (1817-1904): Analysis of British Policy and Activities (1985),* P. K. Jha argues that, Sikkim became a constituent unit of India in 1975, but her political involvement with India started in early 1817 when the Treaty of Titaliya was signed between Sikkim and the British East India Company. However, he says 'Sikkim's political entity was decided by the Lhasa convention of 1904 between Great Britain and Tibet which settled the affairs of Sikkim as affairs of India'. Her merger with India was simply a matter of time.

Sunanda K. Datta-Ray in *Smash and Grab: Annexation of Sikkim (1984),* argues that the merger of Sikkim was not a merger but an annexation. He says that an article which came out after the death of Chogyal in 1982, proves this point, in *The Voice of Sikkim,* "Palden Thondup Namgyal, Chogyal of Sikkim, died more of a broken heart than of throat cancer". Datta-Ray has reached to the micro details of the events that took place in Sikkim during the time of its merger. He has tried to look from the perspective of Durbar and from the perspective of sympathisers to the Durbar.

A. C. Sinha's *Sikkim: Feudal and Democratic (2008),* it has been discussed that the historical studies of Sikkim that exist today deal mostly with invasions, raids and military exploits and also on the British in Sikkim. Normally, a study of such evolutionary processes does not require a strictly chronological treatment. But the history of Sikkim suggests that with certain dates not only the rulers were changed, but also the process of socio-economic and cultural intercourse was dramatically reoriented.

Documents on Sikkim and Bhutan edited by S. K. Sharma and Usha Sharma (1998), is a very useful source for the study. The original documents on Sikkim given in this book is extremely helpful for the researchers, especially those who work on Sikkim. This book has a collection of various treaties, agreements, covenants, deeds, letters and so on signed/exchanged between the British government and the then Rajahs of Sikkim and Bhutan.

Suresh Kumar Gurung's, *Sikkim Ethnicity and Political Dynamics: A Triadic Prespective (2011)* focuses on the developments taken place after the establishment of Namgyal Dynasty in 1642. He has given the historical account of such developments, ranging from 1642 to 1715. In 1817, he mentions after coming in an official pact with the British, what circumstances led to the suspension of the treaty due to the misunderstandings between British India and Sikkim, which led to the treaty of Tumlong in 1861 which made Sikkim finally a British Protectorate state. Coming along in a chronological order, he mentions the developments taken place under various monarchs and he mentions with the withdrawal of the British from India, the treaty signed between India and Sikkim (in post-independent era) strengthened the relation between Sikkim and India. This book also discusses the identity, how ethnic groups in Sikkim exerted their identity in terms of political gain and economic opportunity.

The photographic record of John Claude White (1883-1908) compiled by Kurt Meyer and Pamela Deuel Meyer, *In the Shadows of the Himalayas: Tibet, Bhutan, Nepal and Sikkim (2005)* where the photos taken by Claude White and other officials have been posted along with the vivid descriptions. The author starts with a beautiful remark that being studied in the classical central European tradition, "we studied the Roman and Greek cultures in depth but scarcely studied the rich cultures of Central Asia, South Asia and China." He further adds, in colonial times more than 20 million were scattered across the world as settlers, administrators, merchants and soldiers. The military and political leaders were the key players in determining the fate of the British, all over the world. The practical-minded men whose dogged determination and efficiency made Empire run smoothly. The strategy in Sikkim was to bring the border areas under the firm control of the British Raj.

Tulsiram Sharma's *Sikkim: Hija Dekhi Aja Samma;(From Yesteryears to Today) (1996)* where he gives the vivid description of the history of Sikkim not only after the establishment of Namgyal Dynasty in 1642, but since the Lepcha rulers in the thirteenth century. He says, Lepcha had a simple material culture. They had a subsistence life of hunting and collecting. Some of them had a primitive form of slash and burn type of rotational cultivation of rice, maize and millet. The village was the most important territorial unit in their social system. Some of the influential village headmen assumed the leadership of respective clans. To avoid inter-clan and inter-tribal feuds, they used to negotiate inter-tribal marriage with Limbus, the Magars, the Sherpas, the Bhutias and the Dukpas.

After the establishment of Namgyal Dynasty 12 Namgyal rulers ruled Sikkim which has been vidvidly illustrated by the author. The question of Darjeeling going to the micro level he has given a clear picture of what happened when, in a course of more than 600 years. His main concern is on the political developments in Sikkim, where he has illustrated very clearly the events, developments that took place after the India's independence in Sikkim. As Sikkim was under the protection of India, anything that happened in India had a great impact on Sikkim.

One of the articles used in this study is *The Unification of India, 1947-1951(1951)* by Holden Furber, where he says 'only Bhutan was considered as outside the international frontier of India, after the end of British rule in India, now both Sikkim and Bhutan are outside that frontier'. He further says, the whole apparatus of treaties, paramountcy, princely autonomy and autocracy, and the princes' special status in international law and British constitutional law have been swept away after the end of British rule in India.

Alex McKay's *Tibet 1924: A Very British Coup Attempt? (1997)* where he says Political Officers in Sikkim was responsible for the British relations with Tibet, Sikkim and Bhutan. Most of his work concerned with Tibet. Another article is *Himalayan State Formation and the Impact of British Rule in the Nineteenth Century (1985)* by Richard English where he presents an overview of the cultural and economic history of the Himalaya. The growth of trans-montane trade, the development of intensive agriculture, and the distribution of ethnically diverse populations throughout the region are tied to the formation of successive Hindu and Buddhist states. Of central concern are the processes by which the region was integrated to the colonial economy of British India during the nineteenth century.

Urmila Phadnis's *Ethnic Dimension of Sikkimese Politics: 1979 Elections (1980),* where she says the autochtonous group of the Lepchas had been sandwhiched between two migrants groups – the Bhutias and Nepalis. India was no longer imperial power. The event which led to the merger of Sikkim was the Sikkim National Congress's (SNC) allegation that 1973 eletion was rigged by Durbar.

Another article is *Bhutan and Sikkim: Two Buffer States (1959)* by Werner Levi where he says, at one time or another Bhutan, Sikkim, Tibet, China and Nepal had some special relationship with Britain. If today India and China want to justify their policies in the Himalayas on historical grounds, they can do so with great ease merely by going back into the history to the point, most favourable to their cause.

All these books and articles and documents have given useful information and insights for the current study. By using this, an effort has been made in this book to bring the information together to make some fresh idea/knowledge on the issue discussed. As said by Aloysius, "the past is an explanation of the present" (Aloysius 1997/1998/2008: 3).

The Rationale and Scope of the Study

A number of studies have already been published on Sikkim's early history. However, these studies are focused on early state formation, seventeenth century religious history and some aspects of the British and Indian periods. There are many areas which are yet to be taken up by the researchers and therefore, Sikkim is still a virgin area for the researchers. It is very clear that much work remains to be done even on the period of British influence in the region (Anna Balikci-Denjongpa 2011: 22). According to Anna Balikci, works published after the 1894 *Gazetteer of Sikkim* and the 1908 *History of Sikkim* failed to say anything new as none were based on original research making use of primary sources, with one exceptional work of A.K.J. Singh's *Himalayan Triangle: A Historical Survey of British India's Relations with Tibet, Sikkim and Bhutan 1765-1950* (1988), which made use of the India Office records held at the British Library (ibid: 13). P. R. Rao's work *India and Sikkim: 1814-1970* (1972) can also be added into this category, as it is primarily based on British archival materials.

This study is an effort to fill this important gap by making use of the local sources in local language as well as archival materials. Local sources include the archival materials held at Sikkim Archives and the interviews conducted with experts on the region like journalists, academicians, policy makers and religious scholars. The Archives of Sikkimese Royal Palace was transferred in 2008 to the custodianship of the Namgyal Institute of Tibetology (ibid: 14). These Archives have been used in this work, from the book compiled by Saul Mullard and Hissey Wongchuk, *Royal Records: A Catalogue of the Sikkimese Palace Archives (2010)*. This collection of legal documents, letters and internal and international agreements is a rare source of information for the study of Sikkimese, Tibetan, Bhutanese and British

Indian history. This collection covers a range of historical periods, from the time of early Sikkimese state formation in the mid-seventeenth century[27], the Sikkim-Gorkha war of the 1780s and 1790s, the British period from 1817 till 1947, to the period prior to the merger of Sikkim with India. The collection also contains documents written in a number of different languages including Tibetan, Lepcha, English, Nepali and Mandarin. Similarly they range in format, from letters, treaties, decrees and land grants to personal note books, receipts and private letters. Earlier one of the key problems with conducting historical research in Sikkim was lack of accurate and authentic records which has been minimised with the transfer of this collection (ibid: 14-5).

This study seeks to provide answers to some relevant questions such as, after the signing of Treaty of Titaliya, most of the territories of Sikkim were left with Nepal and the areas around Titaliya though regained from Nepal and Titaliya itself was not handed over to Sikkim, rather East India Company kept it in their own possession. This study seeks to provide an answer that, British followed the policy of acquiring the allegiance of Maharajahs, of what were termed as princely states, allowing them to retain a degree of autonomy while holding tributary status and cooperating with the Company in trade and natural resources. In case of Sikkim, Sikkim was never a princely state of British India rather treaty signed between Sikkim and British India made it an ally and subsequent Treaty of 1861 made it a protectorate state, and soon after the independence of India, Sikkim was not even tried to integrate into India.

---

[27] The earliest document is dated 1663.

Another issue that it interrogates is that, the end of East India Company was not only the result of bloody revolt of 1857, but also the over power play of the British officials in India, which British Government could not afford due to their international consideration and had to bring British East India Company to an end. Alex McKay also talks about this. The most important scope of this research is that it looks into how Sikkim's position vis-à-vis British India was of 'colonial periphery'. The existing popular knowledge and the views of the some scholars and intellectuals are, Sikkim was colonised by the British, it was a colony of British Empire. It is because of the fact that, everything was controlled by the Political Officer at Gangtok, and the Rajah had no say on it. But this research takes a position that Sikkim was never a colony of Britain and was never colonised by Britain, rather Sikkim was a 'colonial periphery' of Britain and it acted as a buffer zone, along with other Eastern Himalayan states between British India and China and Russia.

Organisation of the study

The **objectives** of this study, are; a) to examine Sikkim's relation with Great Britain in colonial period and its impact on the region; b) to identify the factors that shaped the relationship between Sikkim and Great Britain; c) to analyse the significance of Sikkim in the Great Game in Central Asia and; d) to find out why the British discarded their relation with Sikkim after 1947 and transferred the control of Sikkim to independent India.

Questions the study poses are; what impact the British had on Sikkim's political developments? and How does

Sikkim as a peripheral state in the colonial system interacted with the British, an imperial state?

This study follows, Historical-Analytical Method and trying to answer to the questions raised through a detail study of various historical developments that led to the present politics in the region. The source materials used in this study are; books, articles, documents, treaties, agreements, covenants, letters, deeds, *sanads*, documents from Ecclesiastical Department, Government of Sikkim, web-links, religious dictums, bulletins etc. Interviews taken with the experts in the region like journalists, academicians, policy makers and religious scholars having useful knowledge on the theme. And, archaeological sources; stupas found in Sikkim, sculptures, stone carved paintings were also used as sources. Literary evidences and oral history has also been used in this research to substantiate some arguments and verify certain facts.

CHAPTER II

Sikkim and the Great Game in Central Asia

The scope of this chapter is to evaluate the geo-strategic significance of Sikkim and its significance as a crucial link between India and China, and South Asia and Central Asia. This chapter also examines the geopolitical rivalry over Central Asia in the nineteenth century between big powers and the transportation routes (Silk routes) between the two global powers; Russia and Great Britain (Abilov 2013: 30), and China to some extent. The chapter begins with an examination of the key concept of *The Great Game*. Lately, it will analyse what policies these big states pursue in order to impose their political influence to ensure economic benefits.

The *Great Game* has to do with the colonial and strategic rivalry between the Russian and British Empires for the supremacy in Central Asia during nineteenth century. This led to the creation of Afghanistan as a buffer state. Arthur Connolly[28] was the first who coined the phrase, 'The Great Game'[29] in a letter to a friend (ibid: 27). The intrigues for

---

[28] An intelligence officer of the British East India Company, (http://en.wikipedia.org/wiki/The_Great_Game)

[29] However, today, the term is often used to describe the strategic competition for access to oil and gas resources in the Caspian

control of Central Asia at the end of the nineteenth century played out between the two countries which became known as the Great Game (Meyer 2005: 17). For centuries, Central Asia has been the object of rivalries and machinations by the Great Powers. During the nineteenth century, Britain feared that another European power might take the opportunity of the control of Central Asia. With the defeat of the French commercial interests on the subcontinent and Central Asia, Britain gradually acquired control over vast regions of subcontinent and Central Asia (ibid: 15). Although Arthur Connolly is considered to be the creator of the term *Great Game,* it was the writer Rudyard Kipling, through his novel *Kim* (1901), popularized this concept[30].

The question why is it necessary to discuss Sikkim in connection with the 'Great Game' in Central Asia is significant. Various commentators of geopolitics tend to frequently resort to the term *New Great Game*, within the framework of the events that currently took place in Central Asia. *The Great Game* of nineteenth Century, which will be the focal theme of this chapter, in which the British Empire opposed the Russian Empire for the control of Central Asia[31] and stopped, the Russian Empire from penetrating into India, where Sikkim occupies an important position and therefore, Sikkim was strategically important in the plans of

---

region since the break-up of the Soviet Union. This competition is now between Russia, the EU, the US and, more recently, China (Kiernan 2013: 2).

[30] *Central Asia and the Great Games: Different Times, the Same Game?*. Retrieved on January, 15th 2014: 3, url: rc41.ipsa.org/public/ Madrid.../duarte.pdf

[31] ibid: 1

Great Britain. The British considered India as their "Jewel in the Crown" (Bondarevsky 2002: 44). It has been argued that the notion of Great Game is a myth nourished by novelists and analysts of geopolitics. It is important to deconstruct the myth in order to give the actual account of the Great Game[32].

Bondarevsky in *The Great Game: A Russian Perspective* (2002: 1) says 'the battle for the control over Central Asia, Near East and Middle East was fierce and bloody'. It should be noted that Russia and England never declared open war on each other; rather they fought a proxy war making alliances with the local warlords. Despite of avoiding the open war on each other, but still Britain and Russia remain the main players in the Great Game. During the early 19th century when Russia took possession of number of Khanates[33], it generated alarm in the British Government in India and was forced to take steps to protect their colonies in India. That initiated the Great Game between Russia and Britain, for the defence of East India Company's colonies[34].

That resulted in the dispatch of secret agents, exploration missions to the region to facilitate British penetration in an area where the Russian enemy was moving ruthlessly, which led to the development of the region's cartography[35].

---

[32] ibid: 2

[33] Khanates are the Tribal Chiefdoms – Khanate or Khaganate – is a Turko-Mongol word used to describe a political entity ruled by Mongol King, (https://en.m.wikipedia.org/wiki/khanate)

[34] *Central Asia and the Great Games: Different Times, the Same Game?.* Retrieved on 15/01/2014: 4, url: rc41.ipsa.org/public/Madrid.../duarte.pdf

[35] ibid

Britain was aware that if Russia established its control over Central Asia, it would be easy for it to penetrate into India, which British considered their 'Jewel in the Crown'. Therefore, due to its geo-strategic position, Central Asia was the ground for intense rivalry between Britain and Russia. There was an argument that the intention of the Great Game was not only Central Asia, it was a gateway to Afghanistan and India (Abilov 2013: 32). The Central Asian states were pawns of great powers as they compete for power and position[36]. The British believed that Russia would take the possession of Afghanistan, before it takes over India. For Russia, controlling Afghanistan and the neighbouring regions were important step in getting access to the warm waters of Indian Ocean. As a result, the Russians conquered the territories that would later give birth to Kazakhstan, Tajikistan, Turkmenistan and Uzbekistan[37].

From the British point of view, the control of these areas was essential to ensure the protection of all Indian colonies. Due to this concern, Britain declared the First Anglo-Afghan War (1839-1842), one of the first and the most important conflicts of the Great Game. But British failed to establish a regime favourable to their political interests that resulted in a humiliating retreat from Kabul, though this status quo remained for some time, but Afghanistan never ceased to

---

[36] Smith D. L. *Central Asia: A New Great Game?* Retrieved on 22/11/2013: 1, url: http://www.jstor.org/stable/30172401

[37] *Central Asia and the Great Games: Different Times, the Same Game?*. Retrieved on 15/01/2014: 4, url: rc41.ipsa.org/public/Madrid.../duarte.pdf

be a key element in the strategy of British against Russian expansionism[38].

The Great Game was conducted in secret, sometimes in public (Bondarevsky 2002:1) by the two imperial powers in the territories located between Russian and British Empires. The Great Game involved three main phases. The first phase began with the expansion of the Russian Empire in the Caucasus and Central Asia in the late eighteenth and early nineteenth centuries, by generating alarm signals in the East India Company, the *de facto* power in India. The methods used were resorting to secret agents, combined with overt military action. This first phase of the Great Game ended in 1907 with the signing of the Anglo-Russian Convention. The second phase of the Great Game started from 1907 to 1917. The methods used were same as in the previous phase[39]. The third phase of the Great Game took place after the Russian Revolution of 1917, British in India never came up of the 'Russophobe' and ensured every possible means to eliminate Russophobe from Tibet (McKay 1997: 412).

For centuries, Central Asia has been at the crossroads of Eurasia, it is the meeting point of four civilizations that have been controlled by the Central Asian people. According to Xiaojie Xu, "the civilizations that dominate the region have been able to exert their influence in other parts of the world". Central Asia is an inner region, surrounded by a huge land mass that covers a vast territory of steppes, deserts and mountains, occupying an area larger than Western Europe and about half of the United States. The survival

---

[38]   ibid: 4-5

[39]   Ibid: 5

of Central Asian states depends mainly on the maintenance of several corridors and vital connection links according to Xiaojie Xu. With regard to international geopolitics, Central Asia is one of the most important regions of the world, given its impact on the politics and economics of the Great powers. The purpose of the Great Game was based on the geopolitical and imperial domination of the region, through direct administration, hegemonic influence or favorable ideological alliance. The causes of the Russian-British rivalry are still the subject of contention among historians says David Fromkin[40].

Anglo-Russian Rivalry and Eastern Himalayan States

The geopolitical and geo-economic significance of the Eastern Himalayan States played a crucial role for drawing the attention of the regional and global powers in order to dominate the region and impose their political will upon these states (Abilov 2013: 33). It became the subject of interests for various scholars who were dedicated to the study of Eastern Himalayan region; history and development of these states, the role of the Silk route in the trade in Asia and the power rivalries over the control of this region etc. However, there are limited numbers of publications available to find out the significance of Eastern Himalayan states as a geographical area vis-à-vis the power rivalry between England, Russia, and China.

Information from the India Office Records[41] says that the British contact with Tibet, Bhutan, and Nepal can

---

[40]   ibid: 5-14

[41]   India Office Records in the British Library at London hold the

be traced back to eighteenth century, but it was not until the nineteenth century that the documentation of Tibet and its neighbouring countries proliferated which is the result of its involvement in the *Great Game*. Four of the Eastern Himalayan states were engulfed in the Great Game namely; Sikkim, Bhutan, Tibet and Nepal. The records also indicate that from the eighteenth century to early nineteenth century, several attempts were made by the British East India Company to open up trade relations with Tibet, without much success. The most notable exploration of Tibet in the earlier period was made by William Moorcroft, Superintendent of the Bengal Army of the East India Company, who travelled to Tibet in search of fine breeding of horses in 1812. As the Anglo-Russian rivalry in Central Asia intensified by the mid nineteenth century, the British recognised the strategic position of the Eastern Himalaya and tried to make it into a buffer zone against Russian influence[42].

The Eastern Himalayan region occupies a central position in the South Asian landmass and this geographical possession was important because of connecting traditional East/West and North/South trade routes (ibid). At the same time, this region possesses vast amounts of natural resources. Tibet was a conduit for Chinese silks and teas, as well as a source for valuable shawl wool, dyestuffs, and medicinal plants. The British saw the control of trans-Himalayan trade

official documents of Indian affairs in Colonial times. It contains treaties with other states, agreements, letters, deeds and other miscellaneous documents.

[42] Retrieved on January, 17th 2014, url: www.bl.uk/reshelp/findhelpregion/asia/india/indiaofficerecords/indiaofficehub.html

as a means of gaining access to untapped markets in the North. Hard pressed to meet their commitment to unload British broad cloth in India, the Company's Directors suffered substantial losses in having to pay silver bullion for Indian cottons, gauzes, and silks which they exported to England. In this era, when the overseas trade with China had not yet developed, Hastings, then Governor General in the end of eighteenth century, saw the great opportunity in introducing British goods into China via Tibet and Sikkim (English 1985: 70).

Under the instruction of Lord Curzon, the Viceroy of India (1898-1905), an expedition led by Colonel Younghusband was sent to Lhasa in 1904, which came to be known as Younghusband Mission. The purpose of the Mission was to secure a trading agreement and to prevent Tibetans from establishing a relationship with the Russians. While negotiating with the Russians on one side, the British also actively encouraged a *de facto* semi-independence of Tibet, to break away from the 'suzerainty' of China. After the Lhasa expedition of 1904, British established more regular relations with Tibet through the Political Officers in Sikkim, Trade Agents at Gyantse and Yatung, and various British Indian missions to Lhasa[43], which has been discussed in this chapter.

One of the main reasons that the Britain, Russia, and China involved in the political rivalry in the Eastern Himalayan region was due to access to rich resources, control of trade routes and the transportation routes that transfer the resources to the world market (Abilov 2013:

---

[43]   ibid

34). Sikkim figured prominently, as the trade link between Indian sub-continent and the heartland of Asia (Grover 1974: 177). Nevertheless, access to the rich resources has been considered the main reason, but it was not the only motive that great powers engaged in the rivalry. All three powers had political and security interests in the Eastern Himalayan region. Himalayan kingdom of Sikkim occupied a significant position in view of its geopolitical implications. Its strategic location gave it an importance irrespective of its size. It stands at the cross roads of the world, wedged in between, Nepal on the west, Bhutan on the south-east, China on the north and north-east and Darjeeling district on the south (Hunter 1887: 483). England saw this region as an important area for its geo-political strategy, as it connected its position with regard to Tibet, China and Russia (Abilov 2013: 34). Strategically, the position of Sikkim is such for it, it was on Lenin's classic route of communist conquest, he said; 'the road to Paris lies through Peking and Calcutta' (Grover 1974: 177).

Russian concern was an easy passage to the heartland of British Colonial Empire, as such the strategic location of Sikkim was referred as 'a mountain highway to Calcutta' (ibid), through the route from Gyantse in Southern Tibet, crossing across Chumbi Valley to Sikkim and onward India. The second route followed from Shigatse in Tibet to Sikkim, and from Sikkim to Darjeeling and finally to Calcutta (the official heart of British India at that point of time). These two routes were critical for the trade between Sikkim and Tibet, but they also posed a threat to the British because these routes provided potential passage to India, essentially slipping through the India's back door (Meyer 2005: 19).

Chinese concerns were the ethnic and territorial disputes in the region as China wielded suzerainty over Tibet, which was viewed by the British forward group as a strategically critical in guarding the northern frontier from Russian infiltration and control. In reality, Tibetan geopolitics also involved another key player, China (ibid: 17), following the death of Dalai Lama V and the struggle by rival Buddhist sects to claim their reincarnate successors, a struggle brewed which resulted in Chinese assuming suzerainty over Tibet from the early 1700s onward (English 1985: 67). It is also important in this connection that, by the end of the nineteenth century, the British recognised Chinese suzerainty over Tibet (Meyer 2005: 17).

Sikkim and Tibet in the Great Game

The small mountain kingdom of Sikkim had the economic blessing and military misfortune to be located on the two most accessible natural routes between Tibet and India. The players in the Great Game – England and Russia – had the advantage of having only one major pass to conquer[44]. Sikkim was a key strategic outpost in the Great Game where a firm British presence was deemed essential. The Maharajahs' of Sikkim had loyalty to Tibet, and to China

---

[44] Sikkim was strategically deemed important in the chessboard of *The Great Game* between England and Russia. The position of Sikkim is as such that if any power had strengthened its position over Sikkim then it would have advantage over another. Sikkim had a major pass, both in and out through Sikkim of which both the power wanted to take an advantage. In this case Britain became successful in holding position in Sikkim.

as the suzerain who wielded protective power over Sikkim, which was a long-rooted historic fact. The Maharajas' annual payment of the symbolic token gifts to the Chinese emperor is the evidence of the subservient relationship to China (ibid: 20). From the Sikkimese Palace Archives, many documents relating to this regard can be identified. One such document, PD/6.3/003, indicates the unusual case of gifts and letters being returned to the Sikkimese Chogyal by the Chinese Amban (Mullard 2010: 145).

In the late 1800s, the British had to assume that in case of conflict, the Maharajah of Sikkim would be a potential friend and an ally of the Tibetans. One such conflict brewed in 1886 when the Tibetans constructed a fort at Lingtu in the Nathang Valley, 12 miles inside the Sikkimese border. The Tibetans justified their actions as on their own border (Meyer 2005: 20). The fact that Tibetans occupied the Lingtu early in 1886, when the Macaulay Mission under the leadership of Colman Macaulay, then Finance Secretary to Bengal Government, was assembled at Darjeeling with the aim to open up Tibet for the trade. All the details of the Mission were published in the British newspapers and that information soon reached to the Chinese government. The Viceroy of Szechuan province, under whose special direction Tibet was placed, was alarmed at the British usurpation of Upper Burma, and being ignorant of the British intentions in Tibet thought it was desirable to despatch certain number of troops into that country so as to guard against a surprise (Rao 1972: 76).

In Tibet, the news of the Mission caused alarm. Both the Amban and the Viceroy of the Szechuan province reported to the Chinese government, the Tibetan opposition of the

Mission. An influential Tibetan Lama on a visit to Peking informed the Viceroy Li Hung Chang that the Tibetans were opposed to the British Mission as they feared that their territory and religion would be interfered with. The Viceroy calmed the fears of the Lama and told him to use his influence to obtain a commercial and trading facility for the British Indian subjects, and to find a certain place where they could exchange merchandise. The Viceroy felt that a small escort of ten members would be "more likely than a larger one to forward the objects of the Mission" (ibid: 76-7).

The Mission did not start immediately as in February 1886, the Amban at Lhasa was recalled and the new Amban was not expected to join soon. Meanwhile, the news spread that the Tibetans had decided to oppose it. The Tibetan determination to oppose the Mission came to surface when Jongpen of Phari refused to receive from the Maharajah of Sikkim, the communication of the Government of India to the Tibetan Government, intimating the date of the Mission's departure. The Jongpen refused to receive the communication on the ground that he was under strict orders from Lasha not to allow any communications or persons to cross the frontier. Meanwhile, further news was received that the Tibetans had assembled their army on the frontier. Macaulay proposed to the Government of India that the Mission should advance to the Sikkim-Tibet frontier and should hold discussions with the Tibetan frontier officers. He stated that his views were supported by the Dewan of Sikkim, who was a pro-British, who had attributed that the Tibetan opposition to the Mission was due to the failure of the Amban at Lasha to fulfil the instructions from his

Government, as he had no influence over the Tibetans due to his impending departure. Macaulay further informed the Government of India, that the Sikkim Dewan had offered to proceed in advance to Tibet to explain the monks the pacific intentions of the Mission (ibid: 77-8).

Macaulay further suggested to the Government of India to use, when the Mission had reached the Sikkim-Tibet frontier, the services of the Maharajah of Sikkim, Thotub Namgyal, to secure a preliminary interview with the former and the Tibetan officials at Phari. In case the Maharajah declined, or was unable to affect this, Macaulay proposed that he should sit down at the border, demand an interview with the Amban, issue a proclamation in the Tibetan language containing the text of the passport, distribute largesse and await the result. Macaulay wanted to push the Mission across the frontier at any cost, since he was the brain behind the Mission. The Government of India asked him to stay at Darjeeling and wait for the further orders (ibid: 78).

While the Mission stayed idly at Darjeeling, many other developments had taken place. As mentioned briefly earlier, then Viceroy, Dufferin had attacked Upper Burma in late 1885, a country with traditional ties with China (ibid: 78-82) and in January 1886 he had officially annexed it (Singh 1988: 210). He was, therefore, anxious to obtain the Chinese recognition of this annexation. But China, taking advantage of the British anxiety, secured the countermand of the Macaulay Mission. In return, China agreed to recognise British rule and supremacy over Burma, to enter into a Trade Convention, and take steps to promote and stimulate trade between India and Tibet. On 26th July 1886, Dufferin telegraphed the Secretary of State, Lord Kimberley, to say, 'I would not hesitate a moment in sacrificing the Tibet mission for settlement' (ibid) and the Mission was countermanded by the British Government. The failure of the Macaulay Mission, and particularly Tibetan advance after its withdrawal, however, brought into focus two major flaws in the British Treaty with Sikkim of 1861 namely; the non-definition of the *de jure* status of Sikkim and the privilege granted to the Maharajah to stay for three months in a year at Chumbi Valley in Tibet. No sooner the Macaulay Mission had been abandoned, the news came that the Tibetans had advanced into Sikkim across the Jelap La and occupied a place called Lingtu on the Darjeeling road. The Government of India thought that the Tibetans had resorted to that action due to their fear of the Macaulay Mission and hoped that they would withdraw on learning about its abandonment (Rao 1972: 82).

The Tibetans showed no signs of withdrawal from their position at Lingtu, even when they learnt that the Macaulay Mission had been abandoned. Instead they took steps to consolidate their position by building a fort at that place. The Maharajah of Sikkim, Thotub Namgyal, who was then staying at Chumbi Valley, supported the Tibetan action and said that the land in occupation really belonged to Tibet (ibid: 83.) and said; "it had been given to Sikkim because the people of Sikkim had suffered and been much reduced in number, and if, we failed to maintain the independence of the land, Tibet were compelled to assume possession of their own property" (Namgyal 1908: 87).

To prevent further mischief, the Government of Bengal reminded the Maharajah that his support to Tibet was a violation of Articles 19 and 20 of the 1861 Sikkim

Treaty[45] with the Government of India. He was therefore asked to return to his capital. The Maharajah paid no heed to the advice. At last, in December 1887, Maharajah Thotub Namgyal returned to his Kingdom. His return was an indication that he had realized the consequences of disregarding the warnings of the Government of India. In March 1888, a force of about 2,000 men under the command of General Graham took the field. A. W. Paul and J. C. White were attached to it as Political and Assistant Political Officers. The force encountered little opposition and on 21st March 1888 it took Lingtu after a brief clash with the Tibetans. This was the first time when the Tibetans had clashed directly with an army of Western power (Rao 1972: 84-93). The invasion and claims of Chinese suzerainty over Sikkim prompted the Government of India to annex the entire Kingdom as a protectorate in 1889 (English 1985: 73), the Office of the Political Officer was established in Sikkim who was entrusted with the responsibility as a representative of the British in Tibet and Bhutan also, as mentioned earlier.

As already mentioned, Sikkim was deemed essential to establish a firm British presence, as it was a key strategic outpost in the *Great Game,* guarding the Russian and Tibet/Chinese interests in the region. The occupation of the Lingtu Fort by the Tibetan force gave the British a chance to revise the Treaty of 1861 with the Maharajah. The defeat of the Tibetans convinced the Chinese that if they failed to come into terms with the British they might lose their influence in Tibet (Rao 1972: 96). And, in the wider sphere of diplomatic

---

[45] See Annexure: III

necessity it was necessary to establish friendly relations with China, in the face of Russian advance in Central Asia (Singh 1988: 210). As a result, the Convention of 1890[46] took place between Great Britain and China. Both Tibet and Sikkim were kept outside the Convention, though the fate of the Tibet and Sikkim was decided in the Convention. In that Convention, the British secured their position in Sikkim and China recognised validity of Treaty of 1861 fully, and Maharajah's visit to Chumbi Valley was curtailed, instead, he along with the royal family was kept in house arrest in Kalimpong. After the removal of the Maharajah to Kalimpong, John Claude White was appointed as the first Political Officer and posted at Gangtok to look after the administration of the state[47]. A representative Council was selected from the leading men of the state to assist him in the administration (Rao 1972: 100).

The Anglo-Chinese Convention of 1890, was followed by a protocol between the two countries regarding trade, communication, and pasturage which were signed at Darjeeling in December 1893. This convention gave the right to the British for establishing a trade mart at Yatung on the Tibetan side of the frontier. The Convention and the subsequent Trade Protocol had been negotiated over the head of Tibet and Sikkim. Since Tibet was not a party to either of them, it tried to sabotage them by throwing in difficulties, their

---

[46] See Annexure: IV

[47] The Political Officer of Sikkim had the responsibility to look after the administration of Sikkim. He was also responsible for the British relations with Tibet and Bhutan and most of his works was concerned with Tibet, and he was the Government of India's principal advisor on Tibetan affairs (McKay 1997: 412).

implementations. China then was in no position to compel the Tibetans to honour her commitments to the British. She was herself weak and withering (Kotturan 1983: 76-7).

With regard to the demarcation of the boundary line between Sikkim and Tibet, the Tibetan government was singularly uncooperative. They frequently violated the border, and once occupied Giagong claiming that it fell under their territory, they were pushed back. Then Viceroy, Lord Curzon, wanted to bring an end to the continuing uncertainty with Tibet. There was the increasing clamour of the Russian influence gaining a stronghold in Tibet (Kotturan ibid: 77). As China had become weak, she was not in a position to confront with the British, as a result of that, Tibet turned to Russia and sought help, in case of British hostility, they would help them. Lord Curzon came to know that, 'the Tibetans shared a suspicion that the British had designs on them and absorption of Sikkim confirmed them that Tibet was on the next agenda' (Singh 1988: 237). This prompted Tibetans to sought help from Russia and they tried to establish a relation with Russia. This prompted Lord Curzon to send an expedition to Tibet, to have negotiations that they do not have any grand design on Tibet and they do not intend to annex any part of Tibet. British also wanted to chalk out Russophobe from Tibet and open up long awaited chapter of trade relations with Tibet.

The Younghusband Mission and End of Russophobe from Tibet

Lord Curzon was insistent that every indication pointed towards Russian emissaries having access to the Tibetan authorities, and Russian merchants freely traded at various trade marts in Tibet (Singh 1988: 237). When Viceroy was making fruitless efforts to enter into direct communication with Dalai Lama, it came the information that Dalai Lama had been sending an envoy to the Czar Nicholas II[48]. At the head of the mission was the Lama called Dorjieff, and its chief object was rapprochement and the strengthening of good relations with Russia. It had been said that the team was equipped by Dalai Lama and despatched with autograph letters and presents to His Imperial Majesty. And, among other things, it was to raise the question of the establishment of a permanent Tibetan Mission in St. Petersburg for the maintenance of good relations with Russia (Younghusband 1910/1994/2002: 67-8).

Dorjieff, it appeared from an article in the *Novoe Vremya*, 1901, was a Russian subject, who had grown up and received his education on Russian soil. He was by birth a Buriat of Chovinskaia (in the province of Verchnyudinsk, in Trans-Baikalia, Eastern Siberia), and was brought up in the province of Azochozki. He had settled in Tibet twenty years before his present visit to Russia. "This reappearance of the Tibet Mission in Russia proved," said the *Novoe Vremya*, "that the favourable impressions carried back by Dorjieff to his home from his previous mission have confirmed the Dalai Lama in his intention of contracting the friendliest relations

---

[48] British Ambassador at St. Petersburg forwarded to the Foreign Office an announcement in the official column of the *Journal de saint Petersburg* on October 2, 1900, announcing the reception by His Majesty the Emperor of a certain Dorjieff, who was described as first Tsanit Hamba to the Dalai Lama of Tibet (Younghusband 1910/1994/2002: 67).

with Russia. A rapprochement with Russia seemed to Dalai Lama the most natural step, as Russia is the only power able to frustrate the intrigues of Great Britain" (ibid: 68).

The British Indian Government's failure to establish trade marts in Tibet and to establish direct relations with Lhasa was the indication of its failure to safeguard its interests against Russian designs on Tibet. Before Curzon's arrival, the real issues which confronted the British India Government had been frontier disputes over trading facilities. After Curzon's arrival they became inextricably involved with the much wider question of Anglo-Russian rivalry in Asia. Curzon used the three pillars, the Tibetan encroachments at Giaogong and the obstructions imposed on the trade at Yatung, as well as every insult – real or imagined – which British officers had received from the Chinese or Tibetan functionaries, as weapons in his armoury for the "epic struggle"[49] (Singh 1988: 237-38). Curzon's policy was that, nowhere along the Indian glacis should hostile influences be permitted to obtain a foothold, on the contrary British authority should be 'unmistakeably and indeed ostentatiously asserted'; the policy should be to persuade Tibet to ally herself with Britain rather than with Russia (ibid: 238).

Russian government on the other hand, disclaimed the visits of Dorjieff having political nature (Younghusband 1910/1994/2002: 68-9). Curzon was alarmed by the rumours of various treaties which Russia was making with Tibet, and the Russians were in a process of establishing a

---

[49] Younghusband Mission was termed as "epic battle", British was going to open up Tibet for the first time ever since the time of Warren Hastings in later half of the 18th century. Every means were failed till now and they were keen to open up Tibet.

protectorate over Tibet. For Curzon, these rumours were one aspect of the crisis, the other more important sign being the visits of Dorjieff to Czar bearing with him tokens of esteem and friendship from the Dalai Lama. By 1902, Curzon was convinced that Dorjieff was after all a Russian agent of some importance (Singh 1988: 243).

At the same time, the Viceroy was inclined to believe the rumours emanating from China regarding a Sino-Russian treaty over Tibet, and which was said to have been signed at Lhasa on 27th February 1903, by the Amban and a Russian Representative. The treaty was said to contain eight Articles, all dealing with Russian mining rights in Tibet and which gave the Chinese the right to be consulted on every venture the Russians proposed to initiate in Tibet. Moreover, the treaty was to remain valid in the face of protests from other foreign powers (ibid).

By the end of 1902, the India Office, the Foreign office and the Viceroy were all in agreement that reports of Russo-Chinese treaties could no longer be ignored if British India's interests were to be preserved (ibid: 244). The Government of India, accordingly, recommended prompt action. The attempts to negotiate for an understanding with the Tibetans through the Chinese had been proven failed (Younghusband 1910/1994/2002: 76).

Sikkim as an Intermediary in the Younghusband Mission

In July 1903, Colonel Younghusband, along with Mr. Nolan, the British boundary Commissioner, Mr. White, Maharajah Kumar Sidkeong Namgyal and 200 armed men proceeded towards Khambajong, where they saw Kuchap Chief Tungyik and the Tsarong Dapon from the Tibetan side. During the course of the trade negotiations being held there, the Maharajah of Sikkim, Thotub Namgyal wrote a letter to the Tibetan officials in the following strain:-

> "the British Government regarded the articles regarding trade as why important one, if the two governments were to fall out it would cause much misery and woes. The fear lest the dispute between the two Government may assume serious aspect and end in war causes anxiety to us. I therefore beg you who are come to negotiate this affair to assume the peaceful tone, and allow the trade mart at Yatung to be pushed at least as far as Rinhengang in Trome. If you yield that much point you reasonable demand a permanent treaty that will not seek to push it any further. If that be obtained it would be the most desirable and successful issue you could never hope to get. From my humble and ignorant point of view I regard it so, and sincerely wishing the peace and prosperity of our own coreligionists I beg to submit this opinion. I call again upon all the Tutelar and guardian Deities to bear witness to the sincerity of my statement. Therefore I again implore you to do your best in procuring a friendly and permanent peace, which will be the menace of securing the peace and comfort of many souls and saving them untold miseries" (Namgyal 1908: 128).

Nolan had promised Maharajah that his previous power which was held by British Government since his exile will be restored. In reply to the Maharajah's letter, the Tibetan officials wrote, 'that the Tibetans were patiently trying to do their best to preserve peace, but it's British Government who invade and trespass the Tibetan territories, so often, that it is not likely to occur peace between the two governments'. However, they further said that they have sent the Maharajah's letter to the Government and if Government agrees with it, they will forward it to the Maharajah (Namgyal 1908: 128; Singh 1988: 248).

The negotiation at Khambajong failed, and the party went up to Phari via Tromo. The Tibetan Officers in command were Lhading Depon and Namsayling Dapons, the Tibetan troops were at Guru. The party tried to reach out at a fruitful negotiation, but the Tibetan Officials here also discarded the arguments set out by White and the party (Namgyal 1908: 128). White advised Maharajah to write a letter to Dalai Lama, assuming it may produce the better results. Resultantly, Maharajah wrote to Dalai Lama, in usual ornamental fashion:

> "the Omniscient Providence of all sentient beings including the Devas etc. etc. From Your Holiness's humble Client, the Ruler of Sikkim. Most humbly prayeth. With regard to the negotiations going on regarding boundary demarcations and the trade route questions, I have informed Your Holiness's Officers sent down for the purposes that the British Government is building new houses, and opening a new road through bhutanese

territories right up through Gnatong to Phari which shall be passable for carriages. The Government is very powerful and I am very anxious about the safety of our sacred Faith and Church, which might suffer great injuries from them in future. Even if Your Holiness be relying upon Russians for aid, they will not be in a position to render timely aid. If the peace is not made at Yatung, the British are talking of proceeding on to Shingatsi or Gyantsi, and if the matter is not concluded there then they will proceed right up to Lhasa in which case it will be a serious matter. Therefore I beg to suggest that Your Holiness had better allow the trade mart to be shifted from Yatung to Rinchengang and the route be opened a little further up, and get them to sign a treaty binding themselves to desist from seeking to push in any further. I invoke the Jinas and Jina-puttras of the 10 directions to witness. In the disturbance between the two powerful Governments, the Sikkim people have to make roads and carry loads right up to Phari, which is very tiresome work. If the disturbance continue for some years more, the Sikkim subjects will be scattered. The Tutelary Deities know that I am stating truth. So I beg your Holy Omniscience to regard it as such" - Dated: 3rd January 1904 (ibid: 129).

The reply came in the same void, the Dalai Lama wrote,

> 'during the former trouble too, His Holiness's
> (Maharajah) representatives had been left un-
> noticed and that everything had been done
> just to suit the interests of the Chinese and
> the British, while the Tibetans had been
> ignored altogether'. He further said, that,
> 'they had first trespassed unlawfully towards
> Khambajong and had now taken possession of
> Phari Jong. We have thus far borne patiently
> with their affronts, because they are strong
> and we are weak. But henceforth, if they
> continue to act as they have done all along,
> we will be compelled to retaliate step for step,
> just as they do to us' (ibid: 129).

Dalai Lama asked the Maharajah to negotiate on his behalf and try to persuade the British mission to return to Yatung, where the Chinese and Tibetan representatives would be awaiting to settle terms for peace. As per the boundaries, the Dalai Lama maintained that they would have to be settled in accordance with the terms of the treaty enacted in the name of the Chinese Emperor. He also had a word to say about Curzon's accusations regarding Russia, 'we know that they are in manners, customs, caste and creed just the same as the British, and we have no idea of forming such an uncongenial alliance as that of the yak and the pony' (ibid).

The Maharajah appealing the Dalai Lama to come into terms with British Government time and again, was because of the fact that, Maharajah knew if Tibet did not come into terms with the British then they would have to face a humiliating defeat and have to agree on the conditions imposed by the British, because Tibet did not match the military superiority of the British. And, Maharajah was worried about that they would have to actively participate in the tiresome affairs of war, if Dalai Lama's reluctance prolonged the war which they had no option to ignore. Every people in Sikkim were involved in the war, including Maharaj Kumar and Maharajah himself, they were not allowed to flag. Their work was to carry the shipment to the British. But the Maharajah's requests did not yield any productive results, due to the fact that Dalai Lama considered the Maharajah as an agent of British Government, and he brought British to their doorsteps.

Throughout the mission's advance, Sikkim Durbar was pressed into making roads and laying bridges from Rangpo via Lachen and Lachung road and towards Khambajong. A further road from Gangtok to Nathu La, right on to Chumbithang and Shashima was personally supervised by Maharaj Kumar, who, however unwilling to do but had no option, but to do White's bidding. 'Everyone in Sikkim, including the Maharajah, Kazis and Thekedars had to be up and alert at their work. No one was allowed to flag and all had to suffer the intense cold, drenching rain and danger for the whole time up to 1904 until at last it ended' (ibid: 132). And all this was done in the service of the British Government. It was a far cry from the days when Maharajah Thutob Namgyal had chosen to defy the Political Officer and refused to acquiesce in British plans for Sikkim. Now he found not only himself but also his son having to assist in an act of war against the state's traditional suzerain, Tibet. China was weak and without its military backing, Maharajah recognised that, Tibet would be unable to withstand the British pressure. The unwilling acceptance of the Royal Family and the people of Sikkim in decisions which affected their ancient allegiance were indicative of the position of Sikkim as a protectorate after the 1890 Convention, and also of the extent that the British imperial power in the states on the Himalayan periphery (Singh 1988: 247-8).

As the months went by, the Sikkim Durbar found itself committed increasingly to a war in which their old friends, the Tibetans suffered a fatal reverse (ibid: 248). The strength of the Sikkim Military Police was increased by 20 temporary men and was accorded to the supply on loan of 20 carbines and bayonets and necessary accessories with ammunition for the 20 temporary men, on the condition that these would be returned to the Fort William Arsenal, when the services of the temporary force will be dispensed[50].

According to Peter Hopkirk (1997: 10), "Tibetan troops were massacred by the British en route to Lhasa". The massacre at Guru in March 1904, where 700 Tibetans lost their lives after they had agreed to give up their arms, the Maharajah decided to plead, once again, so that he would not be forced to make a humiliating peace. In fact Maharajah had argued that the 'British had not the least intention of depriving Tibet of even an inch of land, upon that they are ready to sign a bond. But they insist on having free trade and friendly interchange of correspondence' (Namgyal 1908: 130).

---

[50] See Annexure: V

The reply, when it came, stated that 'the establishment of trade marts and the opening of new routes into Tibetan territory was something difficult to get the people to agree to that, in the face of their general resolution to the contrary. And since European imports are coming in from India right up to Lhasa, there is no reason why they should insist on establishing trade marts for that purpose because it is the same whether they have marts or not, their things come in all the same'. In Dalai Lama's opinion, the British were bent on 'over-reaching' the Tibetans by actual acts of lawlessness and unprovoked aggression (ibid: 131), and he was left with no alternative but to defend Tibet (Singh 1988: 248).

When Dalai Lama learned that the escort was on its way to Lhasa, he fled the country, the Amban said; 'this was true, and he was evidently not flying to China, but to the north to Urga' (Younghusband 1910/1994/2002: 281). But, before leaving the country, he had said to the National Assembly in written, that; 'the English are very crafty people, and to be careful in making an agreement with them, and to bind them tight'. He further added that he himself would go away and look after the interests of the faith. 'His departure was not regretted by Tibetans' (ibid: 279). Amban said, 'the Ti Rimpoche would act as Regent, and would use the seal which the Dalai Lama had left to him, and this seal would be supported by the seals of the National Assembly of the Council, and of the three great monasteries' (ibid: 293).

On 7th September, 1904, a Convention was signed between British government and Tibetan Government. In the summarized form of the agreement, the following are agreed; the placing of a Resident at Lhasa, or failing that, an agent at Gyantse, with the right to proceed to Lhasa, the formal recognition of exclusive political influence, indemnity of Rs. 75 lakhs to be paid by Tibet, occupation of the Chumbi Valley as security till the amount is paid, the establishment of trade marts at Gyantse, Yatung, Shigatse, and Gartok and the settlement of Sikkim and Garhwal boundaries, Customs duties, and trade regulations[51] (ibid: 260).

The treaty which Younghusband had signed at Lhasa came into certain scrutiny and British Government brought drastic changes to the Convention. On account of Tibet's inability to pay the war indemnity, the Chinese government agreed to pay the reduced indemnity[52]. In an Imperial Decree issued in November, 1905, it was ordered that the 'indemnity should, in view of the poverty of the people, be paid by the Chinese Government' (Younghusband 1910/1994/2002: 348).

Younghusband was the precursor of the forward school of thought who believed in the expansion of the British territory. By that time the forward group had come into power in England. Lord Curzon, then Viceroy, also belonged to the same school. The occupation of Chumbi valley till the amount is paid was done with an intention to annex that part of territory, carved between the Sikkim and Bhutan as it posed a threat to the British interests in Sikkim. Younghusband was cautioned not to place any agent at Lhasa but made a condition that under certain

---

[51] See Annexure: VI

[52] A Telegram to Viceroy, by the British government, said; 'The Viceroy should reduce the indemnity from 75 to 25 lakhs and it should be paid in three instalments', hereby, the British occupation of the Chumbi Valley will be terminated (Younghusband 1910/1994/2002: 338-39).

circumstances Agent at Gyantse would proceed to Lhasa. This clause came into severe scrutiny and was removed because that would commit them to political control over Tibet. The indemnity was also reduced from 75 lakhs to 25 lakhs and China agreed to pay that amount on behalf of Tibet. China did so because China did not want any part of Tibet to be occupied by the British, which may threaten their interest in Tibet.

On April 27th, 1906, a Convention was signed at Peking between Great Britain and China which confirmed the Lhasa Convention of 1904. In addition to that, Great Britain agreed not to annex Tibetan territory, or to interfere in the administration of Tibet, while the Chinese Government undertook not to permit any other foreign State to interfere with the territory or internal administration of Tibet. It was also agreed that, the provisions in the old Convention of 1890, and the Trade Regulations of 1893, should remain in full force[53] (ibid: 342-3).

By this Convention between Great Britain and China, it was clear that the Conventions of 1890 and 1893 would remain in full force. It is important to note that, in both the Conventions; Tibet and Sikkim were not the parties, though matters relating to them were decided in the Conventions. Tibet agreed to abide by the clauses of both the Conventions which they were reluctant to accept before Younghusband Mission, on the ground that Tibet was not a party to the Conventions.

By such an act, it would be conceived that Great Britain and China were exercising their power to the extent, which

---

[53] See Annexure: VII

they thought right. By the Conventions of 1904 and 1906, 'affairs relating to Sikkim were also solved as affairs of India. Lhasa Convention of 1904 gave every assurance to the British and with this the process of establishing British suzerainty over Sikkim was complete in every respect' (Jha 1985: 1). In the Convention of 1906 between Great Britain and China, China ultimately confirmed the suzerainty of British over Sikkim and the confusions in this regard were completely cleared.

On the following year, an agreement was signed between Great Britain and Russia and this Convention – Anglo-Russian Convention – officially brought the *Great Game* to an end (Hopkirk 1997: 10). Many scholars are of the view that, the first phase of the *Great Game* in Central Asia came to an end with the Anglo-Russian Convention of 1907. In the Convention, the suzerain right of China over Tibet was recognised, but, considering the geographical position of Great Britain, it was decided that, Great Britain retains a special interest in the maintenance of the *status quo* in the external relations of Tibet. Both parties agreed to respect territorial integrity of Tibet and to abstain from all interference in its internal administration. Secondly, it is also agreed, not to enter into negotiations with Tibet except through the intermediary of the Chinese Government[54] (Younghusband 1910/1994/2002: 378).

This agreement was neither to exclude the direct relations between British Commercial Agents and the Tibetan authorities provided for in Article V of the Convention between Great Britain and Tibet of September 7th, 1904,

---

[54] See Annexure: VIII

and confirmed by the Convention between Great Britain and China of April 27th, 1906, nor was it to modify the agreements entered into by Great Britain and China in Article I of the Convention of 1906. Rather, this Convention was for the confirmation of Russia on the Conventions of 1904 and 1906, which Great Britain signed with Tibet and China. And, the two governments agreed, not to send their representatives to Lhasa, and they further agreed neither to seek nor to obtain, whether for themselves or their subjects, any concessions for railways, roads, telegraphs, and mines, or other rights in Tibet, and no part of the revenues of Tibet, whether in kind or in cash, were to be pledged or assigned to Great Britain or Russia, or to any of their subjects (ibid: 379). After the signing of the Anglo-Russian Convention, both the governments agreed, not to interfere in the internal affairs of Tibet, and the suzerain right of China over Tibet was recognised by both the governments. Tibet to some extent was secured from the interests of Great Britain and Russia, and was held secured under the suzerainty of China, since any negotiations with Tibet would have to go through China.

Conclusion

After the departure of Younghusband from Lhasa more regular relations were established between the British and Tibet through the Political Office in Sikkim which ensured the diplomatic presence of British in Tibet[55]. Although,

---

[55] The Trade Agents were nominally charged with the protection of the interests of British Indian traders, as Indian Political Officers, their real priority was to exclude Russian influence from Tibet, in

many scholars says that, the Great Game was ended with the Anglo-Russian Convention, but, for British in India they never came up from the 'Russophobe'. That is the reason why, particularly, Lord Curzon wanted to place a British representative at Lhasa, but British Government did not permit him to establish a permanent diplomatic mission at Lhasa. It was the responsibility of British officials in Tibet, as Trade Agents, to stop Russian influence from gaining stronghold in Tibet (McKay 1997: 412).

The Trade Agents in Tibet were under the immediate command of the Political Officer in Sikkim. Most of his work was concerned with Tibet and he played the role of the Government of India's Principal Advisor on Tibetan Affairs (ibid). In Gangtok, Charles Bell became the Political Officer (ibid: 413) after White. Maharajah of Sikkim requested then Viceroy, Lord Minto, 'to grant an extension of the service of White for at least 2 to 3 years more (Namgyal 1908: 140). By then good relations had been occurred between Political Officer and Maharajah, after the misunderstandings of 1890s which led Maharajah to exile in Kurseong, on the British side.

The British officers thought that China's power was a potential threat to the security of India, and they sought to ally with the Tibetan leadership against the Chinese (McKay 1997: 413). While Tibet was too large for Britain to protect militarily, a southern Tibetan state could have been supported, which would have provided a forward position for British interests beyond the Himalayas[56], and had the

---

order to ensure the security of India's northern border (McKay 1997: 412).

[56] The Indian Foreign Secretary Louis Dane had seen that the

potential to be drawn within the frontiers of British India in due course.[57] After O'Connor and Bailey had left Gyantse, and with the Chinese increasing their control over Tibet, the British position declined to the point to withdraw. But in 1910 the Dalai Lama, who had briefly returned to Lhasa, fled south into India to escape a large body of Chinese troops which had been sent to enforce control in Central Tibet. The Dalai Lama's unexpected arrival in India gave the British officials the chance to cultivate a friendship to the traditional Lhasa leadership (ibid: 414).

The Political Officer in Sikkim, Charles Bell, was responsible for the affairs of Dalai Lama when he was in exile. Bell was able to establish a genuine personal friendship with the Tibetan leader. In 1911, the Chinese revolution weakened their position in Tibet and subsequently, Dalai Lama returned from exile and issued what the Tibetans regard as a declaration of independence. Bell offered Dalai Lama such help as his government would permit, and acted as his Principal Advisor on secular matters such as the modernisation of Tibet. Bell supported Dalai Lama's

---

Panchen Lama might be the solution to the Tibetan problem. Dane suggested that if the Panchen Lama took the place of the Dalai Lama in Lhasa with Chinese approval, then the British could recognise Chinese authority in Tibet and settle the Tibetan matters and exclude Russian influence. When Dane looked at the historical precedents concerning the Chinese deposition of 6th and 7th Dalai Lamas, he considered the possibility of Panchen Lama could be an Indian Ruling Chief (McKay 1997: 414).

[57] Tibet at that time had few of the key indicators of modern statehood; it had neither fixed boundaries, nor an indigenous leadership in administrative control of its territory, citizens and foreign relations (McKay 1997: 414-15).

rule, advancing policies based on support for the traditional power structure in Tibet, and the Tibetan leader followed his advice. Bell established what was to be the predominant British policy towards Tibet until 1947, that of support for the Dalai Lama and his Government (ibid: 415).

Bell worked closely with the Dalai Lama, and, as Curzon and Younghusband had envisaged, the presence of a Political Officer at Lhasa enabled the British to exert a great deal of influence there. When Bell departed, Anglo-Tibetan relations were at the most cordial level. Bell retired as Political Officer of Sikkim while he was in Lhasa and F. M. Bailey took over as Political Officer in Sikkim (ibid).

Bell had reported from Lhasa that "there is no danger of Bolshevism in Tibet" as it was antithetical to their religion and culture. Bailey, however, took a different view. He, like O'Connor and many other senior officers of the Raj, believed in a Russian threat to India, not perhaps by invasion, but by subversion, and considered it a duty to fight that threat. There were attempts by the new Russian regime to gain influence in Tibet in the 1920s (ibid: 16). The third phase of the Great Game had started, when Russian agents were dispatched to Lhasa among pilgrim parties from the Russian Buddhist regions, and a Russian agent was despatched in Lhasa's biggest monastery, Drepung. He had his own informants among the Russians, in particular, the Kalmyk Buriat leader Zamba Haldenov, described as "Chief Buddhist priest of the Astrakhan Kalmucks" (ibid: 17).

When Bailey took over as Political Officer in Sikkim, he had been out of contact with Tibet for more than a decade. It became apparent to Bailey that the existing Tibetan Government would not make the changes in Tibet which

British interests demanded. Most particularly, the Tibetans were unwilling to strengthen their military forces, to the extent necessary if Tibet was to act as a strong buffer state for British India's northern frontier, one capable of excluding Russian influence (ibid).

In the *Great Game,* the British were successful in keeping Russian influence away from the states bordering India which includes Sikkim. Be it in Afghanistan or in Eastern Himalaya – particularly in Tibet and Sikkim – British countermanded the influence of Russian Empire and secured their interests by creating a belt of buffer zones on Western Himalaya and Eastern Himalaya. And with the Bolshevism's conquest in Russia which led to the beginning of the third phase of *The Great Game,* British never allowed to materialise Lenin's idea of Communist Conquest that 'road to Paris lies through Peking and Calcutta'. British successfully guarded 'the mountain highway to Calcutta' that is, Sikkim, through diplomatic manoeuvres and military tactics.

CHAPTER III

The Colonial Periphery and the Coloniser: Understanding the Relations between Sikkim and Great Britain

The state of Sikkim was never under direct western colonial rule. It is same in case of other Himalayan states like Nepal, Bhutan and Tibet, though they were all within the influential spheres of colonialism. India was under the direct colonial administration of Britain for more than a century. The modern Indian state is influenced and its institutions are shaped by the colonial system, be it economic or political. In this context, it is important to mention that the effects of being colonised and being in the 'colonial periphery' are largely different. This chapter try to unravel the British influence and its impact on Sikkim by examining various aspects of the relationship between Sikkim and Britain on the one hand and Britain, India and Sikkim on the other.

This chapter analyses the key issues and developments in the relationship between Sikkim and Great Britain. This is done through a critical examination of existing literature on the subject. As mentioned in the preceding chapters, the term 'colonial periphery' has been used to uncover the nature of the relation of Sikkim with Great Britain, which was the major colonial power in the Indian subcontinent. This also aims to position Sikkim in a larger colonial framework for analytical purposes. Sikkim was in such a position where British influence was deemed necessary to protect their colonial interest in India. The geopolitics of the region permitted Sikkim to remain as a 'colonial periphery' but not a "colony". Colonial periphery is a state which is not a colony literally but not outside the zone of influence of the colonial masters. The strategic position of Sikkim was such if Britain had colonised Sikkim and had been made it a part of British Empire then they would have come into a direct confrontation with Tibet/China, which they wanted to avoid and that's the reason why they made Sikkim a 'colonial periphery'.

The four Eastern-Himalayan countries can be termed as 'colonial peripheries' as they were not the colonies of Britain, but subordinated and dependent to the coloniser, as peripheries are dependent to the core countries, for economic and political survival. These states were subordinated to coloniser and were bound by the treaty commitment to coloniser. Any decision of the state had to go through the scrutiny of coloniser. In a way they were landlocked like their positions itself and were under the zone of influence of coloniser, which they had no option to ignore. By creating a zone of influence in the region, the British were protecting themselves, mainly their interest in India.

In this chapter, the relations between Britain and Sikkim have been divided into six phases. With the change in the direction of relations, the relationship enters into a different phase. Each phase has its significance in determining the nature of relationship between the two, and is the result of the interactions between the two. Sometimes relation goes to the extent that, two are the most cordial allies, and at some other occasions, to the sourest that even led to think of pulling out the guarantee given in the treaty. This section of the chapter makes an effort to understand the relationship between the two; one is the imperial power and another, a tiny Himalayan Kingdom, under the shadow of Tibet, by looking on the relationship between the two.

The Early Phase of Anglo-Sikkimese Relationship (1814-1828)

The contact of British with Sikkim can be traced back to 1814 Anglo-Gorkha war. The British contact transformed Sikkim from a traditional monastic state having cultural-religious ties with Tibet to a modern state. The history of its administration can be traced back to 1890s; 'an effort to introduce a rudimentary system of Government on modern lines was made during the time of White' (Sharma 1998: 106). Before discussing the Anglo-Sikkimese relationship in detail, it is necessary to look upon the historical context in which the tiny Himalayan Kingdom, Sikkim, came into contact with the British. 'After the unification of Nepal due to King Prithvi Narayan Shah, Nepal could establish common frontier with Sikkim'[58].

---

[58] The spiritual relation of Sikkim with Nepal is more ancient than the political. Though politically Nepal was fragmented into number of petty kingdoms during the medieval period, some of the kingdoms had relation with Sikkim (Dhanvajra Vajracharya and Tek Bahadur Shresta: "Political Asylum of Kazi Yukla Thup of Sikkim in Nepal": 1, Unpublished Typescript).

By 1780s and 1790s Sikkim came under the pressure of Gorkha expansion on the western part of its territory. In 1788 A.D. Gorkhas invaded Sikkim with an army of about 6,000 men, of whom 2,000 were regulars. 'The whole commanded by Tierar Singh, the Soubah[59] of the Morang. He faced no opposition until he reached the capital. The Rajah ventured a battle in defence of capital, but he was completely defeated owing to the fire of the Gorkha musketeers, who also sustained a considerable loss, yet were successful to besiege the town. All these events took place at some period prior to the 28th of October 1788' (Hamilton 1828: 548).

After experiencing this disaster the Rajah retreated towards the frontiers of Tibet in order to re-assemble an army, and to solicit assistance from the Deb Rajah of Bhutan and the pontiff Lama of Lhasa (ibid). Gorkhas captured most of the Sikkimese territories up to the Teesta river including all of the modern districts of South and West Sikkim as well as Darjeeling. It coincided with the Sino-Gorkha war (1788-1792) (Mullard 2011: 177). The document held at Sikkimese Palace Archives gives the idea that Sikkimese Generals had considerable role in the Sino-Gorkha war. In the document PD/9.5/006, the Chinese Amban writes to the commander of the Sikkimese Army, Yug phyog thub, "to invade Nepal if the Gorkhas invade Tibet", thus opening a second front which the Gorkha army would need to defend, forcing the Gorkha army to fight on two fronts. In the document PD/6.1/004, the "Chinese order the Sikkimese Army to meet with the Chinese General to coordinate the final invasion of Nepal in

---

[59] The Soubah is an officer of justice, revenue and police and the whole revenue of the district was collected by him (Hamilton 1828: 309).

1792" (Mullard 2010: 139). This gives the idea that Sikkimese Generals had played key role in the Gorkha-Tibet war.

In the eventual outcome, Sikkim didn't get the rewards it had hoped for and in fact made considerable losses as a result of the final peace treaty between China and Nepal. The result of this was Sikkim's resentment towards China/Tibet and Nepal and desire to reclaim its possessions (Mullard 2011: 178). 'The affairs of Sikkim continued in this unsatisfactory note till the British's rupture with the Gorkhas in 1814' (Hamilton 1828: 549). The opportunity to exact revenge on Nepal and China/Tibet came with the Anglo-Gorkha war (1814-1816), where Sikkim could reclaim its possessions and ignored Chinese requests to avoid contact with the British (Mullard 2011: 178-79).

The Rajah of Sikkim immediately declared war against Gorkhas, and acted the part of a faithful and according to the extent of his resources, a useful ally to the British. At the pacification of 1815 (Treaty of Sugauli)[60] the Rajah of Sikkim was rewarded by the recovery of a considerable portion of his territory within the hills, to which the Bengal Government added a tract of low land; Morang, ceded by the Gorkhas, to the east of Mechi river (Hamilton 1828: 549). Company did this to strengthen Sikkim as a buffer between Nepal and British India (Rao 1972: 5). The stipulations on which the tract within the hills were restored to the Sikkim Rajah were a cessation of all aggression on his part against the Gorkhas; the employment of his military power and resources in aid of the British troops when engaged among the hills; the

---

[60] The treaty signed between British and Gorkha which brought to an end the Anglo-Gorkha war (See Annexure: I).

exclusion of other Europeans; the surrender of criminals, and the protection of legal commerce (Hamilton 1828: 550).

On the 8th of August 1816 two Chinese envoys of a rank to that of Soubahdar (General) in the Bengal army, arrived at the court of the Sikkim Rajah, accompanied by seventeen others. These persons had been despatched from Lhasa by the Chinese Viziers Tea Chang for the purpose of inquiring if a letter sent some time before by the Viziers to the British Government, had been forwarded to Calcutta, and also to ascertain the existing state of affairs throughout Northern Hindustan. To these Ambassadors the Sikkim Rajah fully explained the nature of his recent connection with the British government, informing them, that although his troops had joined the British against the Gorkhas, the British meditated no hostile movement against any portion of China (ibid).

The Sikkim Rajah has since been the channel through which various despatches have been transmitted from the Bengal government to the Chinese functionaries at Lhasa. The restoration of this state under the British protection and guarantee, constituted a barrier against Gorkha ambitions and eventually hoped, it will lead to the enlargement of British commercial relations with Tibet (ibid). This is the clear point where Sikkim came into direct contact with the British which later moved to the heavy influence of the British over Sikkim. As Rao (1972: 177) observes, "with the signing of the treaty with British, Sikkim started losing its independence".

On 10th February 1817, the British government signed a treaty at Titaliya with Nepal on account of Sikkim. This was signed at the Titaliya Kutchery, the *History of Sikkim (1908)* says, 'the seal of the Mohamedan sovereign was affixed in the document, along with the Governor General's signature.

The territory restored to Sikkim was bounded on the west by Mahanadi, and Mechi river on the east. The Sikkim territory extended from Kanka in the plains along with the Singali La range on the top, to Mechi river in the Terai. The boundaries were demarcated formerly by Major Blatter, the representatives from Sikkim were; Lama Dichen Wangdu, Chinye Tenzing and Machen Tenpa' (Namgyal 1908: 56). Rao says 'Rajah was tempted by the bait of the territory wrested from Nepal to Sikkim, that's why he entered into the treaty'. 'The Treaty of Titaliya marked the beginning of the end of Sikkim's existence as an independent state' (Rao 1972: 177).

Despite the effort being made to ensure no border dispute arose in the Treaty of Titaliya[61], Sikkim Rajah was worried about it[62]. *History of Sikkim (1908)* says; 'Soon after the Treaty of Titaliya (1817) was signed, Mr. Chagzod Karwang the maternal uncle of the then Rajah Tsugphud Namgyal, misappropriated every income to satisfy his own selfish wants by illegally using the state seal. By 1819 things began to assume a serious note, even to the extent of the Kazis and Lamas had to assemble and make peace between the Rajah and Chagzod Karwang. Chagzod Karwang disregarded this agreement. Things did not change and in 1826, Rajah ordered his men to execute Chagzod Karwang' (Namgyal 1908: 58). Article written by Dhanvajra Vajracharya and Tek Bahadur Shresta (Political Asylum of Kazi Yukla Thup of Sikkim in Nepal) says; 'To secure from the attack from Nepal or Tibet, the Rajah of Sikkim in the year 1826 decided to shift the capital to a more secure place. However, the *Dewan*,

---

[61] See Annexure: II

[62] Dhanvajra Vajracharya and Tek Bahadur Shresta: "Political Asylum of Kazi Yukla Thup of Sikkim in Nepal": 2, Unpublished Typescript.

uncle of the Rajah and a powerful man, disagreed with the proposal. The issue led to serious clash of interest between the Dewan and the Rajah. Eventually, the entire family of the Dewan was massacred'[63].

Here, the two different sources are trying to justify the same event and offers their narrations respectively. Both are unpublished secondary sources; one is *History of Sikkim (1908)* and another is "Political Asylum of Kazi Yukla Thup of Sikkim in Nepal" written by Dhanvajra Vajracharya and Tek Bahadur Shresta. One thing is clear that Chagzod Karwang, the maternal uncle of Rajah Tsugphud Namgyal (along with his entire family) was assassinated in the year 1826, and the subsequent political implications are the result of this. The "Political Asylum of Kazi Yukla Thup of Sikkim in Nepal" talks about the shifting of capital to the more secure place, the *History of Sikkim (1908)* has not mentioned about it. It is obvious that Rajah wanted to shift the capital to more secure place, and eventually he did, the capital was shifted to Tumlong.

After the massacre of Dewan's family, his nephew Kazi Yukla Thup along with his family sought asylum in Nepal. With him also came over eight hundred Sikkimese Lepcha's and Limboo's seeking refuge in Nepal. The Nepali Government happily provided asylum to those Sikkimese seeking refuge. The Nepali Government had thought of mobilizing them in two fronts. Firstly to expand the political dominance in Sikkim and secondly, to populate the areas of Illam with these refugees as well those coming in future. With this view, the Nepal Government had provided with

---

[63] ibid.

many facilities to the families of Kazi Yukla Thup. Some of
the royal decrees as written to the Padam Chandra Lepcha,
the progeny of Kazi Yukla Thup by the Nepali Government
are still found preserved[64]. After the Nepal Government
was informed by Officer appointed for eastern Nepal Subba
Jayant Khatri about Kazi Yukla Thup and his followers
seeking asylum after infiltrating to Nepal, the high officials
including General Bhimsen Thapa wrote an approval letter
in 1827. In that letter to Kazi Yukla Thup, it has been
written;

> "we have come to learn that you along with
> your family members and other citizens
> have come here seeking refuge after internal
> conflict broke out in Sikkim, earlier too you
> were of this place, and presently you have
> done wonderful job by coming here along
> with your family and other showing your
> loyalty"[65].

The unpublished article "Political Asylum of Kazi Yukla
Thup of Sikkim in Nepal" (Dhanvajra Vajracharya and Tek
Bahadur Shresta) says; "The Nepal Government had further
intention of extending its political influence in Sikkim even
after the treaty of Sugauli". The subsequent raids on Sikkim
by Lepchas taken refuge in Nepal proves this point, the
Rajah of Sikkim had to sought British help to extradite
those who were causing raids on Sikkim, as guaranteed in
the Treaty of Titaliya (1817). Although Nepal Government

---

[64] ibid: 2-3.
[65] ibid: 3.

had tried to create disturbances in Sikkim with the help of those refugees, it did not yield anything. It is the British Government who could capitalize from that disturbance. In this very context the British Government could get the beautiful and salubrious hill station of Darjeeling from Sikkim[66].

Second Phase of Anglo-Sikkimese Relationship (1828-1835)

The Rajah sought a British intervention to extradite those who are causing raids on Sikkim, since the Rajah was under the treaty obligation with the Company. By this time a boundary dispute had also been arisen between Sikkim and Nepal regarding the jurisdiction over a piece of land called Ontoo, situated on the eastern side of the Mechi river (Singh 1988: 177). The raiding party also sought help from the Company for the support and protection from the Rajah (Rao 1972: 6). The matter was referred to the British Government according to the terms of the treaty. In 1828 C. A. Llyod then Captain and Mr. J. W. Grant I.C.S. were deputed to settle the issues between Nepal and Sikkim. While settling the internal feuds between these two parties, both went to inspect the Sikkim boundary, and came till Rinchenpong. On their way they saw Dorjeling[67] encircled

---

[66] ibid.

[67] Present day Darjeeling – The most important stronghold of the country, as it was selected by the Gorkhas for their principal military station, when Gorkhas invaded Sikkim in 1788 A. D., the Gorkha garrisons were established in Sikkim and Darjeeling, these were the two principal stations of the district (Hamilton

by the forest and they were struck by the idea of suitability of hills, as a sanatorium for Europeans and informed the then Governor General (Namgyal 1908: 61, Bhanja 1993: 2-3, Rao 1972: 7). Lord William Bentick, then Governor General deputed Captain Herbert, a surveyor to examine the place along with Mr. Llyod and Mr. Grant. Their findings suggested that the site would not only make an ideal sanatorium but also confer considerable political benefits for the Company (Rao 1972: 7).

Lord William Bentick then Governor General, thus, proposed to the Council in 1830, that they should open negotiations with Rajah Tsugphud Namgyal for the transfer of Darjeeling to the East India Company. But, Sir Charles Metcalfe, a member of the Council opposed the proposal on the grounds that it would not only rouse the suspicions of the Rajah and eventually involve the British in disputes with him, also the jealousy of the Nepalese who might consider the Company's possession of Darjeeling, so near their frontier as a preliminary step to the British invasion of Nepal. These opinions prevailed and the subject was dropped for the time being (ibid: 7-8).

In 1831, J. W. Grant wrote to Rajah Tsugphud Namgyal regarding the insurrection of the Lepchas under the traitor Yukla Thup; "If we hold an interview about the matter, the insurrection will be suppressed very easily, and you need not entertain the least anxiety about it, I would like to come to Darjeeling to meet you. But it would not be with the intention to take any portion of your land; were that our intention, then where was the use of our restoring the

---

1828: 547-8).

Morang Terai to you formally. The custom or policy of our Government is, when we have once given any land or property, we don't take it back" (Namgyal 1908: 58). However, it is clear that the British were looking Darjeeling as an ideal place for the sanatorium and to install their troops in such a commanding height from where they could observe all the Eastern Himalayan states. In 1832, Smith[68] informed that they would request the Government of Nepal to impose restrictions on the activities of the Lepcha refugees from Sikkim, but at the same time they advised the Rajah to adopt a conciliatory policy towards his refugee subjects (Rao 1972: 6).

At the same time the Lepchas in Illam, under the Gorkha government, were known to be contemplating a raid on the Sikkim Terai (Namgyal 1908: 61). In 1833, Lepcha refugees made another inroad into Sikkim (Rao 1972: 8). The Government of India sent Llyod to inquire into the matter, and 'that compelled the Illam Lepchas to return quietly to their homes' (Namgyal 1908: 61). Lord Bentick wanted to exploit this situation to acquire Darjeeling. He therefore, proposed the Council that Llyod should be deputed to negotiate with the Rajah of Sikkim for the cession of Darjeeling 'in exchange for an equivalent either in land or money'. Once again, the project was dropped due to the opposition by Sir Charles Metcalfe (Rao 1972: 8).

In January 1835, Llyod in a private letter to Captain T. H. Taylor at the Government House, enquired about the government's intention to establish a sanatorium at Darjeeling. He felt that the suspicion of the Rajah of Sikkim

---

[68] The Magistrate of Rungpur.

about the British intentions was the only obstacle to its establishment, but he was sure that it could be removed. The enquiry of Llyod revived the Company's interest in the project. On 8th January 1835, Bentick proposed to the Council that Llyod might be sent to Sikkim to negotiate with the Rajah regarding the transfer of Darjeeling to the East India Company. This time the Council, which did not include Sir Charles Metcalfe, approved the proposal and decided to depute Llyod to Sikkim to negotiate with the Rajah for the transfer of Darjeeling to the Company in exchange for such equivalent either in land or money. Further, he wanted that Llyod should explain to the Rajah that the British interest in Darjeeling was only motivated by the idea of establishment of a sanatorium there (ibid: 8-9).

Llyod left for Sikkim on 8th February 1835, and after travelling ten days he reached Tumlong, the then capital of Sikkim. Immediately on reaching Tumlong, he paid a courtesy call on the Rajah. The next day he again met the Rajah in full Durbar. Before he could request the Rajah for the transfer of Darjeeling to the Company, the Rajah himself made three requests to Llyod. The requests were that; the boundary of his Kingdom might be extended up to Konchi, Kummo Pradhan, the embezzler of the Morang revenues should be arrested and delivered to him and Debgoan might be added to his Kingdom. Llyod pleaded his inability to accede to the Rajah's first request as it was beyond his power. Regarding second request, Llyod did not say anything except expressing the wish that he might mediate between the Rajah and the Lepchas and their Kazis so as to settle their disputes. As to the third request of the Rajah, Llyod did not make any comment except mentioning that the Governor

General desired to have Darjeeling in exchange for lands in the plains or for a sum of money. On hearing this, Rajah informed Llyod that he would give his answer the next day (ibid: 9-10).

The Rajah did not give his answer next day, but sent his officers to discuss with Llyod the different points connected with his requests. It is not known what had transpired at these discussions. On the sixth day of his stay at Tumlong, Llyod met the Rajah for the last time and requested him to give a definite answer regarding the cession of Darjeeling to the Company. On hearing that, the Rajah gave Llyod, a paper with first demand about Konchi having been removed, with two requests regarding the cession of Darjeeling; first was, Kummo Pradhan should be made to account for the embezzlement and restore his plunder and, second was, Debgoan should be ceded. The Rajah further informed Llyod that if his both requests are met, he would give Darjeeling to the Company "out of friendship". The Rajah gave this letter of deed to his officers, while escorting Llyod, on his way back to Darjeeling. The officers were instructed to hand over this document only when his requests are taken into consideration. Llyod, however, succeeded in getting possession of the letter of the deed, found it to be imperfectly drafted. He therefore, drafted a new deed and sent it to the Rajah with a request that this paper should be substituted with a similar paper, for the one Rajah had delivered with his officers (Rao 1972: 10, Singh 1988: 178).

When Llyod sent the new draft to the Rajah, he was perfectly aware that the Company could get Darjeeling only by acceding to the Rajah's requests. This is evident from his letter to the Government wherein he stated that it could obtain Darjeeling by ceding Debgoan to Sikkim and by compelling Kummo Pradhan to make good the Morang revenues to the Rajah. Llyod considered it important to obtain the possession of Darjeeling for reasons other than its cold climate because "as a military post that must stand pre-eminent". He further informed the Government that Darjeeling would be cheaply got in exchange for Debgoan. British Government considered Rajah's conditions for the cession of Darjeeling as impracticable since Debgoan was already given to the Jalpaiguri Rajah in 1828, and regarding the other condition it doubted whether it would be justified in compelling a settlement of accounts between the Rajah and his subjects (Rao 1972: 10-11).

The Company neither arrested Kummo Pradhan nor compelled him to render account of the default. The plea of the Governor General to the Rajah that "it is not consistent with our practice to call people to account for money transactions which have taken place in foreign territories" was not convincing to the Rajah, especially when he suspected that Kummo Pradhan had treasonable intentions of giving away Morang to Nepal (ibid: 11).

The Government, after rejecting Rajah's conditions for the transfer of Darjeeling, asked Lloyd to point out any waste land in the neighbourhood of Sikkim which could be transferred to the Rajah in exchange for Darjeeling. If there was no such waste land, Llyod was asked to give his opinion regarding the amount of pecuniary compensation which the Rajah may consider sufficient in exchange for Darjeeling. Lloyd was unable to point out any waste land, which could be given to Rajah in exchange for Darjeeling. Regarding pecuniary compensation he valued Darjeeling at Rs. 120,000 but doubted its acceptance by the Rajah since he attached little value to money. On hearing this, Sir Charles Metcalfe, the Officiating Governor General of India, ordered Llyod to abstain from further negotiations with the Rajah as he was not "cordially disposed to cede it". On receiving that order, Llyod informed the Government that the "Deed of Darjeeling Grant" was already in his possession[69] (ibid: 12).

Llyod, while on his way back from Sikkim to Darjeeling, sent the Rajah a new draft of the Darjeeling Deed requesting him to "substitute this or similar paper" for the one he had delivered to his officers. The Rajah on receiving that new draft, which was backdated 1st February 1835, affixed his red seal and returned to Llyod. That was the "Deed of the Grant of Darjeeling"[70]. It is important to note that the new Deed was the substitute for the original one which the Rajah gave to his officers with instructions that it should be delivered to Llyod as soon as his requests are considered with. When Llyod received the Deed of the Darjeeling Grant, he was aware that the Government was not going to comply with the Rajah's conditions. In fact he was asked by the Government to refrain from further negotiations with

---

[69] He did not inform the Government of this very important fact as soon as he received the Deed (Rao 1972: 12), the reason could be he did not want Darjeeling to go from their hands as he was the one who talked about suitability of converting Darjeeling into sanatorium for Europeans with Governor General at first. He was allured by the beauty of Darjeeling and would have thought about making the proper use of the Deed in a right time. When right time came he revealed about the possession of 'Deed of Darjeeling Grant'.

[70] See Annexure: IX

the Rajah. The plain course left for him was to return the Deed to the Rajah, but instead of doing that he wrote a letter to the Rajah asking him to mention whether he desired to give Darjeeling to the British Government out of friendship. This action of Llyod not only violated the 15th June, 1835 orders of the Government of India, wherein he was asked to refrain from further negotiations with the Rajah, but also went against the clear mandate of Lord Bentick, who, in his minute of 17th June 1835, cautioned his officers that "the cession of Darjeeling should not be ultimately insisted on, unless the terms offered as an equivalent to the Sikkim Rajah should be really satisfactory to him". Further, Llyod did not send to the Government a copy of the letter he had addressed to the Rajah. The Rajah's reply is on record, it is an important document since it was on receiving, that Llyod considered himself at liberty to make use of the Grant, and forwarded it to the Government who thereupon took possession of Darjeeling. The Rajah's reply was as follows:

> "Your letter and present of a box has reached me and having been understood (sic) afforded me much pleasure. You write that vakeels from Nepaul have arrived, and having been waiting a long time, but that my vakeels have not come and you wish to know the reasons for their delay and request that on receipt of your letter I would despatch them in order that boundary of Siddikola may be ascertained and fixed. You have thus written to me but I am now sending you both the vakeels and have the goodness to settle firmly the boundary for me – and you have also

many times written about Darjeeling, but last
year the grant of Darjeeling under my red seal
was delivered to you through my vakeels and
there can never be any departure from that
by my Government – if you have understood
that differently I cannot help it – continue
to gratify me with your welfare. I send three
yards of Cochin as present" (Rao ibid: 12-13).

This letter was written as a reply to Llyod's letter and
for an answer since he was waiting for a long, to his two
stipulations regarding; ceding of Debgoan and the arrest
of Kummo Pradhan. Rajah enquired as to when the
Bengal Government intended to discharge their part of
bargain. He pointed out that when he had said that the
'grant having been made and he would not depart from
it', he assumed that his terms had already been honoured,
otherwise the cession of Darjeeling was something he would,
on no account, have agreed to (Singh 1988: 179). The
main theme of the letter was in relation to the boundary
dispute with Nepal and the non-arrival of his vakeels from
Sikkim as vakeels from Nepal had already arrived to discuss
matters relating to the boundary dispute between Sikkim
and Nepal. From the Rajah's reply Llyod concluded that
the cession of Darjeeling was unconditional and informed
the Government that the Rajah "makes the grant freely,
mentions no conditions whatsoever and seems to regret that
he has been misunderstood". The Government replied to
Llyod in the following notable terms:

'As it now appears that the transfer has been
unconditionally made by the Raja, it only

remains to consider the best means of turning
it to the advantage of the British Government'
(Rao 1972: 13-14).

One would conclude as Llyod treacherously secured
Darjeeling claiming it unconditional surrender, looks strange
in view of the above mentioned facts. And a letter sent by
Rajah Tsugphud Namgyal in 1843 to the Superintendent,
the British Officer incharge of Darjeeling confirms it not an
act of unconditional surrender, wherein he reminds British
Government of equal compensation to Darjeeling, he writes;

> "Formerly we received a letter from India
> Government at Calcutta saying that the
> Government wanted a piece of land in
> Darjeeling for a Sanitary station for invalid
> British Officers and that either a suitable
> piece of land in exchange or some rent in
> money would be given. Accordingly I offered
> a piece of land in Darjeeling for the purpose.
> The proposed exchange in land was not given,
> but you persisted in offering an annual rent
> in money. And you know clearly, whether we
> sent any one to ask for rent money or not.
> Now you write to say that you will not send up
> the annual rent for the Darjeeling land. Now,
> if you do not live in Darjeeling we do not
> want any money either" (Namgyal 1908: 61).

This shows Rajah's resentment on the annexation of
Darjeeling. Whatever might been the methods of securing
Darjeeling, it had considerable impact on the subsequent

relation between Sikkim and the Company. Darjeeling became the observatory post, and placed themselves in close contact with all the hill states of the Eastern Himalaya and also constantly reminded them, the possibilities of trade with Tibet (Rao 1972: 14).

The British argument of turning Darjeeling into a sanatorium might be a convincing one but they must have looked it from political point of view also. Since, Nepal was very close to Darjeeling, if they station their troops at Darjeeling then Nepal literally would be content to their own border. As Darjeeling was very close to Nepal, the Rajah of Sikkim literally neglected that place and never thought of developing the place for the fact that Nepal was always hostile to Sikkim. Darjeeling was less revenue producing estate with only population of hundred and a dense forest. Llyod visualised immense potential of this place at once (Kotturan 1983: 60) and considered this place would be a summer residence for the Bengal Governor, because of its cold weather. The other reason might be, the age old desire of the British to open up commercial relations with Tibet, for which they saw Darjeeling a suitable trade post. According to Kotturan, Darjeeling's use as a military base for the defence of the trade route to Tibet through Sikkim was apparent. From its commanding height the whole of Sikkim and the neighbourhood would be observed and protected (ibid).

Many scholars, namely P. R. Rao (1972), Saul Mullard (2011) and A. K. J. Singh (1988) are of the view that cession of Darjeeling had a great impact on the subsequent developments in Anglo-Sikkimese relations. The relation till then going on a friendly note, turned into sour after the annexation of Darjeeling. The annexation of Darjeeling, depended upon the interpretation to the letter of Rajah to Llyod. However, in *History of Sikkim (1908),* Maharajah Thotub Namgyal and Gyalmo argues that, then Maharajah offered the Government (British Government) a piece of land of Darjeeling with a letter or deed in 1835 (Namgyal 1908: 61). But it has not mentioned that, it was "out of friendship", it has only mentioned, "a piece of land of Darjeeling was 'offered' to the Government". The events which unfolded after the cession of Darjeeling tell us whether it was a gift or high-handed diplomatic manoeuvres.

The Third Phase of Anglo-Sikkimese Relationship (1835-1861)

The cession of Darjeeling had a lasting impact on not only Anglo-Sikkimese relations which fell into a steep decline after 1835, but also on Sikkim's relations with Tibet, China and Bhutan. Tibetan Government forbade the Rajah to enter into Tibet, if Rajah wishes to enter into Tibet then it would be possible in once, in eight years. As the Rajah violated the order of the China that Rajah should not keep any relation with foreign power, for which China had sent its Amban to enquire into the matter, China got infuriated with the act of cession of Darjeeling and the Chinese and Tibetan Governments' instructions were made through the letter to Sikkim Durbar against the free pasturage of Sikkim cattle and the supply of transport exacted by the Sikkim Rajah, 'Sikkim Durbar required to pay for grasses taken for feeding of ponies and mules, rent for houses, and hire for transport' (Namgyal 1908: 63).

The key factor in the decline of Anglo-Sikkimese relations was the total misunderstanding of what the Darjeeling land grant meant to both the British and the Sikkimese. The British assumed that the land grant meant that Darjeeling had become sovereign British territory, whereas the Sikkimese understood this land grant according to Sikkimese land law[71]. The British failed to understand this and so believed Darjeeling was sovereign British territory, in which British law would prevail and not the rule of the Chogyal[72] of Sikkim (Mullard 2011: 182-83). The site was already occupied by the British on the strength of the Deed. What the Rajah immediately got in return was a gift parcel – one double barrelled gun, one rifle, one 20 yards of

---

[71] In Sikkimese law, land grants were issued to leading families in exchange for an annual rents based on the tax yield of an estate, which could be changed depending upon the annual income of an estate; loyalty to the Sikkimese throne including the recognition of the supremacy of the Chogyal rights over the land and adherence to Sikkimese law (Mullard 2011: 182).

[72] The secular head of the State but also an incarnate lama with responsibility to rule the subjects in accordance with the gist of the *"Chhos"* i.e. Dharma. The basic tenets of the Lamaists policy in Sikkim ever since 1642 was the *Chhos* as the established religion of the rulers (rGyalpo) who were instrumental in upholding the doctrine justifying the designation, 'Chos-Gyal' (Chogyal). In ideological sense, the traditional Tibetan government was a synthesis of clerical and lay elements. "As there were two sets of laws – one for Lha-sde (the domain of the church) and one for the Mi-sde (domain of the state). The monks and the nobles were closely connected and there could not be any absolute separation between spiritual and temporal estates. The apex, the Sakya hierarchy, was the meeting point of both ecclesiastical and civil jurisdictions (Sinha 2008: 39).

red-broad cloth, two pairs of shawls, one of superior variety and the other of inferior variety (Kotturan 1983: 62). The annexation of Darjeeling proved to be of great importance to the British, not only in their relations with the hill states of Bhutan and Nepal, but as a reminder of the possibilities of trade with Tibet (Singh 1988: 180). 'The relations between the Rajah and the East India Company soured as the latter failed to compensate the former adequately for the cession of Darjeeling' (Rao 1972: 15).

The manner of the annexation strained the relations between Rajah and Llyod (Singh 1988: 180), as Llyod was the brain behind the annexation. Llyod was to complain that the Rajah tried to put every obstacle in the way of development of the hill station, particularly in regard to preventing Sikkimese labour from going down to Darjeeling (ibid). The Rajah was embittered with the Company for not receiving adequate compensation for the cession of Darjeeling. Thus, he prevented his people visiting Darjeeling for the purpose of trade and commerce, which retarded the progress of the settlement (Rao 1972: 17). 'The subsequent communications between Sikkim and British about the compensation issue only helped to create bad blood' (Kotturan 1983: 62).

Things did not change until 1839, Rajah did not get anything as compensation/rent. In 1839 Dr. A. Campbell was posted as new Superintendent of Darjeeling and In-charge of Political Relations with Sikkim (Singh 1988: 181). In November 1839, Rajah wrote to Campbell; "Llyod promised that whatever money I should desire in return should be granted, that my territory should be extended west to the Tambar River; that Kummoo Pradhan and his brother should be delivered over to me; and that the deficit in my revenue in their hands should be made good" (Jha 1985: 6). When it came to the question of compensation, 'Superintendent turned unsympathetic and lost no time in disowning the promises made by Llyod' (Kotturan 1983: 62). Campbell replied; "I did not know that you desired more in return for it than the satisfaction of having met the wishes of my Government" (Jha 1985: 6). He further went on denying that, Llyod had ever promised Rajah a land in exchange for Darjeeling. The Rajah thought it wise to address the Governor General, particularly in view of the fact that throughout his negotiations with Llyod, promises had been made to recompense, either with a land or money, nothing had been given (Singh 1988: 181). However, the Governor General was unwilling to reopen the issue which he considered had already been settled (Kotturan 1983: 62). Rajah set out some new demands, since the Company was not prepared to cede back Debgoan, he was prepared to accept a small tract of land lying east of the Mahanadi river and west of the river Teesta (Singh 1988: 181).

Campbell informed the Government that it must show to the Rajah that it was not insensible to the benefits derived through his gift. The Government of India therefore asked Campbell in March 1840 to inform the Rajah that it was not possible to make any territorial grant to him, but that Government is anxious to make yearly payments which will exceed the value of Darjeeling under his Government. The Government felt that Rs. 1,000 a year would be an adequate compensation for the Rajah, but at the same time Government informed Campbell that, it is willing to enhance that amount provided the Rajah if allows, "free

intercourse between Darjeeling and the interior of Sikkim"
(Rao 1972: 17). Here, the Government played a bargaining
card to penetrate into the interior of Sikkim. In terms of
diplomacy Sikkim was nowhere around Great Britain.

After a lot of graceless bargaining, the compensation
was fixed at Rs. 3,000 which was made payable from
1841 (Kotturan 1983: 62). The Government, meanwhile,
informed Campbell that the enhanced allowance may
increase Rajah's "spirit of discontent" since he had again
applied to the Governor General for the cession of Debgoan.
Thereupon, Campbell suggested to the Government that the
Rajah's compensation need not have retrospective effect from
the date of the annexation[73]. The Government accepted that
suggestion and informed the Rajah that he would be paid
the annual compensation of Rs. 3,000 and that the payment
would commence from the date Rajah accept Company's
offer. The Rajah accepted the first and not the second offer.
Campbell however, thought that the Rajah had accepted
the second offer. The Government also took no notice of
this (Rao 1972: 17-8) and amount was made payable from
later 1841, after a long British annexation of the territory.
The Sikkimese became more suspicious of British intentions
(Kotturan 1983: 62).

It is evident in the *History of Sikkim (1908: 61)*, that
Rajah Tsugphud Namgyal in 1843 wrote a letter to Campbell
stating;

---

[73] In September 1841 Rajah accepted Rs. 3,000 as compensation for
Darjeeling and had to wait till June 1847 to get the arrears of the
compensation since 1835 (Jha 1985: 7).

"The original boundary of Sikkim as demarcated by the Major Col. Saheb (Llyod) was from the Manchi (Mechi) river. But since you have come, you have cut the boundary from the smaller Manchi river, and given it to the Gurkhas. In the letter I received from the great Saheb I am informed that Campbell Saheb has sent to further my interests and you yourself wrote to me, informing me of your arrival and assuring me of your wish to further my interests and to work agreeably to my wishes. But in real fact ever since your arrival in Darjeeling you have not only done nothing to help me, but giving ears to all the talks of evil minded people endless disputes have arisen. The neighbouring States are perpetually bothering me. It will not do if Darjeeling falls into another State's hands, or if any of the raiyats of Darjeeling get scattered".

In about a decade's time Darjeeling became a flourishing settlement of more than 10,000 inhabitants. Immigrants came in large numbers to enjoy the freedom of British India from the neighbouring kingdoms of Nepal, Bhutan and Sikkim in all of which slavery and forced labour was prevalent. There was plenty of forest land and every encouragement was given to the settlers. Later large scale plantation of high quality tea raised the economic importance of the area (Kotturan 1983: 62). Rao says, the growth of Darjeeling from an uninhabited place in 1835 to a flourishing settlement of 10,000 people within a decade arose the jealousy of Sikkimese. The presence of a British enclave in the midst of the Sikkim territory created troubles. The troubles also started over the question of the extradition of slaves and criminals who used to escape to Darjeeling from Sikkim. The Sikkim authorities resented the refusal of the British to surrender the slaves who took refuge in Darjeeling. Similarly, the British frowned upon the non-cooperation of the Sikkimese in apprehending British Indian criminals who took refuge in Sikkim. Added to these, there was one more cause of discontent and complaint associated with Campbell. It was the loss of Ontoo Hill by Sikkim. The loss of that area was made a subject of complaint by the Rajah which evidently added fuel to the fire (Rao 1972: 19).

Campbell, on his part, was unable to establish a good relation with the Rajah. Rajah was charged with the act of vexations and warned that if he persisted in his unfriendly course the Government would be compelled to attach his possessions in Morang (ibid: 19-20). In August 1846 Rajah sent his Dewan or Chief Minister Ilam Singh to Darjeeling to reply to the charges of Campbell. Ilam Singh met Campbell on 17th August 1846, and afterwards he had two more meetings with him on 3rd October, and 3rd December 1846. Dewan agreed to allow the British, as it was objected by the British the use of Sikkim lime deposits (ibid: 20-21) at Singmare in Sikkim (Jha 1985: 8). Rajah granted the use of lime deposits at Singmare because Rajah could not stand by the charges imposed by Campbell and had to accede on the charges. The motivations behind these charges could be, Campbell did not have good relation with Rajah and never missed a chance to offend Rajah and whenever British got an opportunity to play its bargaining card they used it and by playing bargaining card they attach of Sikkim possessions.

Campbell informed the Government that with the exception of the matter relating to the southern boundary of Darjeeling, the Rajah had agreed to what was asked in a "proper and becoming manner" and that the matters under discussion were settled. While Ilam Singh was offering explanations to Campbell's charges against Rajah of Sikkim, Government of India reviewed all its proceedings with the latter in connection with and subsequent to the Grant of Darjeeling. It found in Campbell's correspondence with Rajah "a tone of rebuke and superiority". He was therefore enjoined to avoid in future all proceedings and correspondence of a "harsh and irritating nature". Further he was asked to treat the Rajah "not as a dependent, but as a prince who though possessed of little power, is regarded by the British Government as one of its allies". Apart from these instructions to Campbell, the Government of India decided to increase the amount of Rajah's annual compensation from Rs. 3,000 to Rs. 6,000 with effect from 1846, since it found that it had not adequately compensated the Rajah for the cession of Darjeeling (Rao 1972: 21-2) and another reason for this unilateral decision would be Rajah's acceding to the demands of British, they had out of generosity increased Rajah's annual compensation.

Even after the enhancement of the compensation, the relations between Sikkim and British Government did not improve much. The reasons were, firstly the death of Ilam Singh in 1847 (ibid: 22). He was the only man in the Sikkim Durbar who found the possible to negotiate with Campbell and as the only man in Sikkim who could be trusted in word of deed (Singh 1988: 181, Rao 1972: 22). The second reason was the confused state of Sikkim politics. After the death of Ilam Singh, Tokhang Namgyal[74] became the Dewan of Sikkim. His ascendancy was challenged by Lepchas who were led by Aden Chebu Lama. The two factions led by Tokhang Namgyal and Chebu Lama were involved in an intense rivalry over the question of succession of the throne. The Rajah's only surviving son Sidkeong Namgyal was a celibate Lama. As such he was considered ineligible to succeed his father Rajah Tsugphud Namgyal. The only other candidate was the Rajah's illegitimate son, whose sister was married by Tokhang Namgyal. Naturally Namgyal supported the candidature of his brother-in-law, the illegitimate son of the Rajah. The faction led by Aden Chebu Lama was opposed to this. It wanted the succession of the Rajah's Lama son, Sidkeong Namgyal. To remove the difficulties in the way of succession of Sidkeong Namgyal, Chebu Lama in 1848, persuaded Dalai Lama to dispense with the vows of celibacy of the former and also arranged his marriage[75] (Rao 1972: 22-3).

---

[74] Tokhang Namgyal was a Tibetan who had married the Rajah's illegitimate daughter. He used that influence in his rise to power (Rao 1972: 22).

[75] When Rajah came to know about this, Rajah was very angry with him (Sidkeong Namgyal) for two reasons, namely; he said 'the ordained priest should think of marrying' and secondly 'that being born an Avtar Lama he should have thought of becoming a layman by assuming the Raj Guddi'. The Rajah got his ministers to inquire from the princes as to what he had to say about this. At that time it was proved that Tseepa Aden better known as Chebu Lama was the man who caused the rupture between the father and son. The latter was compelled to give a written apology and sign a bond (Namgyal 1908: 65).

In 1848, the British were involved in the internal conflict with Sikkim. In that year, Dr. Joseph Hooker, the distinguished English naturalist, came to Darjeeling to explore Sikkim and the Himalayas. Campbell, with the permission of then Governor General, Lord Dalhousie, wrote to the Rajah to permit Hooker to travel through Sikkim (ibid: 23). The Sikkim authorities flatly refused Dalhousie's expectation that Hooker would be allowed to procure his researches in Sikkim on the plea that no foreigners could be allowed to travel in Sikkim, Campbell presumed the refusal was due to influence of Pagla Dewan[76] who had monopoly in Sikkim's trade with Tibet. After a prolonged wrangle Hooker was allowed to visit Sikkim[77] (Jha 1985: 8-9).

Campbell felt that he could not satisfactorily carry on the business with the Rajah unless he himself had access to him. He therefore obtained the permission of the Governor General to visit the Rajah of Sikkim, as it was the only means of ascertaining real sentiments and feelings of the Rajah. The Government gave the permission, but enjoined on Campbell not to transact any business with the Rajah during the visit. The *Dewan* Namgyal met him on the way and tried to prevent him from meeting the Rajah by giving all sorts

---

[76] Tokhang Dewan Namgyal also used to known as "Pagla Dewan" which means 'insane Chief Minister'.

[77] The correspondence of the Government of India with Sikkim was carried through the latter's vakeel or Agent at Darjeeling. Campbell suspected that his letters had never reached the Rajah, but handed over to the Dewan Namgyal who was opposed to the free travel of Europeans into Sikkim and whose policy was to enter as little as possible with an active alliance with the British (Rao 1972: 23).

of excuses. Campbell brushed aside all those objections and met the Rajah. The meeting was purely in a formal affair as Campbell was instructed by the Government not to transact any business with the Rajah during the visit. Campbell, during his short stay in Sikkim, gained sufficient insight into its politics. He realized that the Sikkimese were "woefully ignorant" and "misinformed" regarding the real nature of the British power in India (Rao 1972: 23-4).

Campbell made his second trip to Sikkim in 1849. It came about like this; Dr. Hooker, who was then touring Sikkim, complained to Campbell that the Sikkim officials are causing him excessive annoyances and obstructions. On receiving that complaint, Campbell addressed a letter to the Rajah of Sikkim asking him to punish the concerned officials. Meanwhile he learnt from Hooker that the Sikkim officials who had caused him annoyances in the Lachen Valley did not fully acknowledge the authority of the Rajah and were in some degree subordinate to Tibet. To understand the causes of obstruction to Hooker's travel in the Lachen valley, Campbell considered it necessary to proceed to that quarter. Campbell, with the permission of the Rajah entered Sikkim in September 1849. He was accompanied by Chebu Lama, Sikkim's vakeel at Darjeeling. On 2nd October 1849 he visited Tumlong, then capital and sent a letter to Rajah asking him to punish the officials who were responsible for causing annoyances and obstructions to Hooker. While at Tumlong, he was met by Hooker. After a short stay he along with Hooker proceeded to the Kangralama pass and entered into Tibet despite the protests from the Sikkim officials and the Tibetan Frontier Guards (ibid: 24-5). The Rajah himself was forbidden to visit Tibet except once in eight years.

Campbell and Hooker returned to Sikkim via Donkya pass[78]. Campbell's entry into Tibet was brought to the notice of the Rajah of Sikkim. The Rajah, who was believed to be in some degree subordinated to Tibet, sent a letter to Campbell when he visited Tumlong again in November 1849, requesting him to return to Darjeeling (Rao 1972: 25). Campbell ignored the letter as he felt that by returning to Darjeeling he would be abandoning his demand on the Rajah for the punishment of his officials responsible for obstructions in the way of Hooker's travels. He wanted to meet Rajah but failed, he then left Tumlong along with Hooker and proceeded to Chola pass and crossed into the Chumbi valley of Tibet which he wanted to investigate as the possible route for Indian trade with Tibet. As soon as they entered Tibet for the second time, they were met by Tibetan soldiers who refused to allow them to proceed further and escorted back to the Sikkim frontier. On reaching the Sikkim territory on 7th November 1849, they were arrested by the Rajah's officials and taken to Tumlong (ibid).

Hooker and Campbell were roughly seized by the Dewan's men. According to Sikkimese lore, Campbell, who was bound hand and foot, began yelling "Hooker! Hooker! The savages are murdering me!" whereupon one of his captors ordered: "If he wants a hookah, let him have one!" 'The unfortunate superintendent was forced to the ground and Dewan Namgyal's own hookah thrust into his

---

[78] The entry of Campbell and Hooker into Tibet was a clear violation of the regulations of that country which had prohibited the entry of Europeans (Rao 1972: 25).

mouth and held there for a considerable time' (Datta-Ray 1984,2004: 25).

The Rajah was so offended with Campbell that he wanted the Governor General to replace him and till this was done and his slaves were restored to him, Rajah wanted to detain Hooker and Campbell (Jha 1985: 9). The Rajah in his letter to the Governor General gave his own version of the arrest of Campbell. In the letter he stated that he allowed Hooker to travel freely in Sikkim, but he did not allow him to cross the Tibetan and Bhutan frontiers. Regarding Campbell he said that he could not receive Campbell as his health was bad but sent him a message that he would be able to see him in two days. As Campbell paid no attention to the message and went to Chola pass, he sent his Dewan with presents to meet him. The Dewan met Campbell on the second day and offered him presents and informed him that it would be dangerous to cross the Chinese and Bhutia territories and implored him not to bring trouble to their country. The Rajah further informed the Governor General that Campbell thrashed "most severely" his servants. From that conduct of Campbell the Rajah was "greatly distressed". He therefore, out of necessity, detained Campbell and Hooker (Rao 1972: 25-6).

Campbell's trespass to Tibet was the cause of his arrest. Campbell on the other hand maintained that his entry into Tibet had nothing to do with his arrest, before he went to Tibet he had fully satisfied himself through Chebu Lama, that the Rajah had no treaty with Tibet and was not bound by any engagement to be the guardian of that country's limits. He insisted that he was arrested as the Rajah wanted to force him to accept Lasso Kazi as his Vakeel at

Darjeeling[79], and to surrender the Sikkim slaves settled at Darjeeling (ibid: 26).

According to Captain Byng, officiating Superintendent of Darjeeling, Campbell brought the mischief upon himself by repeated defiance of the Rajah's wishes and authority "such as no sovereign however insignificant so ever could be expected to endure"[80]. The Campbell's arrest did not result from the miscellaneous official matter alien to his Tibetan visit. Campbell's argument that Sikkim was not the guardian of the Tibetan frontier was not reasonable when we consider the position of Sikkim vis-à-vis Tibet and China. Captain Byng felt that Sikkim ought not to be subjected to the "wrath of China" unless they are prepared to "protect and compensate" Sikkim. In London, the Political and Military Committee of the East India Company regarded "the infringement of Dr. Campbell of the Chinese regulations prohibiting the entry of strangers to their territory was an act of grave indiscretion"[81]. In the light of these views it was difficult to resist the conclusion that the Tibetan trespass had precipitated Campbell's arrest (ibid: 26-7).

The news of Campbell's arrest caused considerable panic at Darjeeling. The Rajah, Tsugphud Namgyal refused to comply with the demand of the Governor General Lord

---

[79] In April 1849 Lasso Kazi, an adherent of Dewan Namgyal, was appointed as Sikkim's Vakeel at Darjeeling. Campbell refused to receive him and successfully insisted upon the appointment of the pro-British, Aden Chebu Lama in his place (Rao 1972: 26).

[80] Letter of Byng to Government of India, 29 November 1849. *F.P.C.*, 29 December 1849: 232 (Rao 1972).

[81] Political letter from the Secretary of State to the Governor-General, 30 July 1851, No. 28 (Rao 1972; 27).

Dalhousie for the release of Campbell and Hooker on the plea that the Governor General's letters did not bear proper seals. To recover its prestige the Government felt it "indispensably necessary" that the "savage insolence" of the Sikkim Rajah "should be severely chastised". It might have happened so that the letters did not reach to the Rajah and it was all dealing by Dewan Namgyal. Company sought to threaten Rajah by sending a letter demanding, the immediate release of the prisoners otherwise they would advance to Sikkim capital and occupy the country. The prisoners were released on 9th December 1849, as the Rajah or precisely the Pagla Dewan was afraid that they will have to face severe consequences as the Company moved its troops to the bank of Rangit river (ibid: 27-8).

The Rajah's annual compensation of Rs. 6,000 for the cession of Darjeeling was stripped. The Company annexed Morang[82], a small tract of land given by the East India Company to Sikkim Rajah. Because of this the Sikkim Rajah was cut off from access to the plains except through the British territory. After effecting the annexations, the Government of India was faced with the problem of whether or not to withdraw the guarantee of security given to Sikkim under the Treaty of Titaliya. If Company withdraws the guarantee given in the Treaty of Titaliya, then it was felt that, Nepal might take possession of Sikkim and would be in a position to render itself very powerful and disagreeable neighbour in the event of any misunderstanding with the British Government. Company believed, the withdrawal of

---

[82] The country to the west of Teesta river up to the junction of the Great Rangit river, and from there the country to the west and south of the Rangit and Rambang rivers (Rao 1972: 28).

the British guarantee would be an invitation to all states; Tibet, Nepal and Bhutan to possess the remainder of Sikkim. Nepal and Bhutan would be at once in the field for the spoil and as the former is the most powerful in arms, she would have it, and after having it a short time would enable her to extend her domination over Bhutan. Nepal in that case would be within ten miles of Darjeeling. It would be then necessary for the British to maintain a huge army to prevent Darjeeling from becoming an insular speck in the immense mountain kingdom of Nepal. Government of India influenced by these arguments, thought it necessary to continue its connection with Sikkim (ibid: 28-9).

It is evident that the crisis of 1849 had brought into focus the real position of Sikkim vis-à-vis the Government of India. When the Company established its relation with Sikkim in 1817, it regarded the Rajah as its ally and afterwards granted him the Morang suitable to that situation. But within three decades and a half, the position of the Rajah was so reduced that he was contemptuously regarded as a "Hill Savage". The decline in the status of the Rajah was the outcome of Sikkim's reduced size and importance. Moreover, by the Treaty of Titaliya, the Company had gained substantial privileges over Sikkim. Not only did Sikkim lose its right of independent action in its disputes with Nepal and other neighbouring states, but it also began to lose its territory bit by bit. In 1835 it was forced to give Darjeeling as a "gift" to Company. By this, though the Company gained a bit of territory, it lost the goodwill of Sikkim. The 1849 crisis resulted in the Company gaining additional Sikkimese territory to the extent of 640 sq. miles. As discussed in the preceding lines, if the Company did not annex the whole of Sikkim, it was because of the political necessity of maintaining that kingdom as a separate entity. Sikkim was not wiped out of the map because of its strategic location between Nepal, Bhutan, Tibet and British dominion in India (ibid: 30-1).

Taking advantage of Rajah's strained relations with the British, ex-Dewan Namgyal who was banished from the country on account of his involvement in the 1849 crisis, came back and began to take a prominent part in Sikkim politics. The Rajah, as he became too old to govern the country himself, retired to Chumbi valley in Tibet leaving the administration in the hands of Namgyal. In March 1859, Namgyal, in the name and with the knowledge of the Rajah, sent a deputation to the Government of Bengal, demanding the payment of the enhanced annual allowance of Rs. 12,000 or as an alternative for the restoration of Sikkim's territory confiscated in 1850[83]. The Government of Bengal viewed this as an affront to its prestige and demanded an apology from the Rajah. The Dewan Namgyal not only ignored the demand, but also prevented his subjects from travelling to the British territories for purposes of trade or labour. This was followed by raids on British territory of Darjeeling. British Indian subjects were carried off and sold as slaves or detained in Sikkim. On 19th March 1860 a grave case of kidnapping was reported to the Government of Bengal. Some 13 Sikkimese raided a British Indian village called Tukdah and kidnapped two women. The raiders eventually turned out to be the relatives of Dewan Namgyal. In April

---

[83] Annexation of Morang district after the arrest of Dr. A. Campbell and Dr. Hooker.

and May 1860 two more cases of kidnapping were reported to the Bengal Government (ibid: 32-3).

Sir J. P. Grant, the Lieutenant Governor of Bengal, suggested to Government of India, to take retaliatory measures, such as the destruction of the Rajah's property or the arrest of his subjects. The Government of India rejected the suggestion to arrest the subjects of the Rajah as it felt that innocent third parties should not be subjected to coercion. On the suggestion of the Government of India, Dr. Campbell opened negotiations with Rajah. While the negotiations were in progress, on 1st October 1860 Campbell sent an ultimatum to the Rajah demanding; the restoration of the kidnapped persons, compensation to those who have been plundered and, the arrest and surrender of the kidnappers and plunderers. The Rajah was warned that if within one month of the receipt of the letter the demands were not complied with, his territory lying to the west of the river Great Rangit and north of the river Rambang would be occupied (ibid: 33).

On the receipt of that ultimatum, Kabi Kaji, a Sikkim official, informed Campbell that the Sikkim Government had decided to depute Chebu Lama, the Rajah's vakeel at Darjeeling to meet him. He therefore requested Campbell not to be displeased till he met Chebu Lama. On 23rd October 1860 Campbell received a letter from the Rajah Tsugphud Namgyal stating that he would not be "playing fool with the British Government". Two days after the receipt of the Rajah's letter, i.e. on 25th October 1860, Chebu Lama met Campbell and informed him that he failed to get the criminals or kidnapped persons even though the Rajah had directed him to call upon his disobedient officers to arrest the criminals and hand over to Campbell. From that conversation Campbell concluded that the Rajah or his advisers had "wilfully and deliberately" ignored the demands of the Government of India. He therefore decided to execute the threat of the occupation of Sikkim territory lying to the west of the river Great Rangit, and to the north of the river Rangit (ibid: 33-4).

On 1ˢᵗ November 1860, Campbell crossed the Rambang river and entered into Sikkim with a small force under the command of Captain Murray and advanced upto Rinchenpong[84]. The difficulties presented by the physical features of Sikkim were immense, as noted by British officials. Campbell reported to the Bengal Government that he had received the "cordial assistance and support" of all classes of population including the officers of the Rajah in all grades. Everything seemed to be progressing most favourably up to the morning of 27ᵗʰ November 1860. But during the afternoon Chebu Lama's spies brought the information that the Dewan intended to attack the British position[85]. The intelligence brought by the Chebu Lama's spies proved to be correct, on the very night of 27ᵗʰ November 1860, the Dewan attacked the British position. The next morning i.e., on 28ᵗʰ November 1860, the Dewan's son-in-law addressed a letter to Campbell asking him to withdraw to Darjeeling. The letter ended with a warning that if Campbell decided to fight, he would see whether the Sikkimese were "men or women" (ibid: 34-5).

Campbell ignored that letter. The next day, i.e. on 29ᵗʰ November 1860, the Sikkimese made another attack with a

---

[84]   It is a place on west Sikkim.

[85]   Here it may be mentioned that the pro-British Chebu Lama was with Campbell since 25ᵗʰ October 1860.

large force and tried to carry the British stockade. When the fighting stopped on the morning of 30th November 1860, the pro-British Chebu Lama came and informed Campbell of the rumour that Darjeeling was attacked. That information tallied with the earlier information Campbell received that Lasso Kazi, one of the adherents of Dewan Namgyal, was intending to attack Darjeeling. Thereupon, Captain Murray, the commander of the British forces, checked the stock of ammunition available with him and realized the "impossibility of standing another attack". A Council of War was held and after considering three points, namely; the non-receipt of the Government reply to their earlier appeal for additional troops and ammunition, the impossibility of holding the position with knives only, and the impossibility of receiving support from Darjeeling, which they had every reason to believe was the case, it was decided to retreat to the British territory (ibid: 35).

The retreat which commenced on 30th November 1860, was nearly a rout. The Sikkimese waylaid the British forces and captured a large quantity of their ammunition including seventy rifles. After marching fifty miles, Campbell reached a place called Goke in the British territory on 1st December 1860. Murray justified the decision to retreat on the ground that it prevented the death or capture of everyone in the stockade. He felt that the capture of Campbell would have placed Government of India in a "most unpleasant position". Campbell also justified the retreat on the same ground (ibid: 36).

The alleged provocation for expedition was the Rajah's non-compliance with the British demand for the surrender of the kidnapped persons. Had Campbell given the Rajah some more time to comply with the demands of the Government of India, perhaps the need for the expedition would not have arisen. The expedition of Campbell gives support to the belief that Campbell wanted to avenge the Rajah for his arrest and imprisonment in Sikkim in 1849 (ibid: 35-7).

The second reason for Campbell's expedition was his belief that the rule of Dewan Namgyal was so unpopular that he would not meet with any opposition to this advance. As a matter of fact, he expected a warm welcome in Sikkim. Sir J. P. Grant was convinced that Campbell's opinion as to the alleged grinding rule of the Dewan and the eagerness of the many people to overthrow it were not well-founded. How thoroughly Campbell was mistaken in his belief was proved by the events of 27-30 November, 1860 when the Sikkimese nearly annihilated the British position at Rinchenpong. Campbell considered the Sikkimese attack as "terribly treacherous". The allegation is entirely baseless. As already noted, on 29th November 1860, i.e. one day before the Sikkimese renewed attack on the British position at Rinchenpong, the Dewan's son-in-law asked Campbell by letter to withdraw to Darjeeling. Campbell ignored the letter and prepared to fight. It looked as though to justify his retreat Campbell characterized the Sikkimese attack as "treacherous" (ibid: 37-8).

As it is clear, Dr. Campbell had played a role in worsening Anglo-Sikkimese relations. As Superintendent of Darjeeling he was in direct charge of East India Company's relations with Sikkim. 'Being a qualified doctor, he was unequal to the task which needed considerable diplomatic skills' (Kotturan 1983: 63). Then Governor General, Lord Canning, could not see proof of treachery in Campbell's reports and did not accept that allegation. Campbell's expedition to Sikkim was uncalled for and it had not solved any of the British problems with that Kingdom. On the contrary, it had complicated them further and forced the Government of India to undertake a fresh military expedition (Rao 1972: 37-8).

The retreat of Campbell from Sikkim was a great blow to the British prestige. The Government of India, therefore, thought it necessary to take immediate steps not only to demonstrate its power and restore its prestige in Sikkim but also to reduce the likely unpleasant political effects upon Tibet and Bhutan. Campbell felt that the immediate objectives of the Government of India in Sikkim should be; the release of prisoners captured by the Sikkimese in their recent attack, enforcement of its earlier demand for the restoration of the kidnapped British Indian subjects, infliction of punishment on the Rajah and security against future aggression and treachery. He therefore informed, the Bengal Government that the above objectives could be achieved by following one of the three alternative policies he had thought of. The first was the permanent annexation of the territory lately occupied i.e. the territory lying to the west of the river Great Rangit and north of the river Rambang with suitable guarantee against future aggression. He however felt, that this would be an "inadequate" compensation, since the area to be annexed is very small. He therefore, as a second alternative suggested that in addition to the territory mentioned in the first alternative, the territory lying between the rivers Great Rangit and the Teesta, should be annexed permanently. Even these annexations, he felt to be "barely adequate". He therefore, as a third alternative, suggested the annexation of the entire Kingdom of Sikkim as it would "secure us all our objects" (ibid: 38).

Campbell wanted that the Government of India should consider his second suggestion in case it did not want to annex the entire Kingdom of Sikkim, on the ground that it would bring the British Indian Empire into direct territorial contact with Tibet. He informed the Government that his second suggestion had the approval of Chebu Lama, who felt that the Government of India by annexing only a portion of Sikkim would be keeping the door open for reconciliation in some form or other with the Rajah. The suggestions of Campbell for the partial or full annexation of Sikkim did not find favour with the Bengal Government. Sir J. P. Grant felt that a partial annexation of Sikkim would not be solving their difficulties with that Kingdom. At the same time he was not in favour of the complete annexation of Sikkim, as it was likely to bring them into difficulties with Tibet. He therefore, suggested Government of India that it should enter into a treaty with the Rajah under which Sikkim was to; keep a Vakeel at Darjeeling, permit the Government of India to make a road through its territory up to the Tibetan frontier, grant waste lands to British subjects, deliver up criminals and restore all kidnapped subjects (ibid: 38-9), again British officials got an opportunity to play their bargaining card and make Rajah accede to their demands.

Government of India accepted the suggestion of Sir J. P. Grant and decided "not to annex any portion of Sikkim to British dominions". But to remove the discredit it had suffered on account of Campbell's retreat and to punish the Rajah, it considered two things as indispensable. They are; the threatened occupation of the Rajah's lands adjoining the British territory was to be made good and, a blow should be struck in the interior of Sikkim by advancing the British forces up to Tumlong (then capital of Sikkim). To attain these objectives, they decided to send a Military Expedition into Sikkim under the command of J. C. Gawler, with Ashley Eden as the Political Officer attached to it (ibid: 39).

The British Expeditionary Force left Darjeeling on 1st February 1861 and met with little or no opposition (ibid: 42). At this time the Rajah Tsugphud Namgyal was at Chumbi with his son and family[86] (Namgyal 1908: 66). Dewan Namgyal fled to Tibet the moment he realized that British troops had approached to the Teesta river. The Rajah agreed to enter into the treaty with the British. On 28th March 1861, at Tumlong the treaty was signed on behalf of the Government of India by Ashley Eden, and Sidkeong Namgyal, the son of Rajah Tsugphud Namgyal, on behalf of Sikkim Durbar. With the conclusion of the treaty, British relations with Sikkim were once again normalized (Rao 1972: 42). The real cause of the misunderstanding which led to the expedition from the British side was traced to Tokhang Dewan Namgyal, who was banished from Sikkim (Namgyal 1908: 67). The treaty consisted 23 Articles, and all the former treaties between the British Government and

---

[86] Political Officer requested either the Rajah himself or his son to meet him in which event a new treaty would be made. The information was conveyed to him by the Lamas and Lay ministers of Sikkim. But Chebu Lama sent up the Phodang Lama purposely to say that if the Rajah's son, Kyabgon Sridkyong came down then the treaty would be favourable to the Sikkimites. This private information from him made the Rajah Tsugphud Namgyal deter from his purpose of coming down in person and sent down his son Kyabgon Sridkyong instead (Namgyal 1908: 67).

Sikkim were cancelled and it was declared that now on Rajah will be referred as "Maha Rajah" (Rao 1972: 42).

The Fourth Phase of Anglo-Sikkimese Relationship (1861-1888)

The fourth phase of Anglo-Sikkimese relation enters with Sikkim as a protectorate of British Government. The British Government did not withdraw the guarantee given in the Treaty of Titaliya, even after the crisis that followed by the detention of Dr. Hooker and Campbell. The fundamental reason was that Sikkim without British guarantee would have become an easy prey of any of the Eastern Himalayan states, most particularly Nepal because it had superior weaponry compared to other Eastern Himalayan states. After the Treaty of Tumlong, the relation entered into stable note, it was not the satisfaction which led to the stability of Anglo-Sikkimese relations, but it was coercion which led to the stable relationship between Sikkim and British India. Sikkim had no choice but to concede its demands to the coloniser. The relation between Sikkim and Great Britain, the former as colonial periphery and the latter as coloniser, was dictated by the terms imposed by British Government upon Sikkim. Sikkim was completely dependent to British India in terms of security, both political and economic[87].

In 1862, Maharajah Tsugphud Namgyal abdicated the throne in favour of his legitimate eldest son Sidkeong Namgyal.

---

[87] After the incident of detention of Hooker and Campbell the Rajah was reduced to extreme poverty as a result of annexation of Morang and elimination of annual compensation for Darjeeling (Namgyal 1908: 66).

The twelve years rule of Sidkeong Namgyal was the happiest period in the British-Sikkim relations. The Government of India as a matter of grace to the Maharajah Sidkeong Namgyal restored the annual grant of Rs. 6,000 which was forfeited in 1850. It was increased to Rs. 9,000 in 1868. In March 1873 the Maharajah Sidkeong Namgyal visited Darjeeling to meet Sir George Campbell, the Lieutenant-Governor of Bengal[88]. The main object of the Maharajah's visit was to request the Government to increase his annual allowance from Rs. 9,000 to 12,000 (Rao 1972: 45). Sir George Campbell recommended to the Government of India to increase Maharajah's allowance. While recommending the increase of the Maharajah's allowances, Sir George Campbell reminded the Government of India that the territories taken from Sikkim were becoming yearly of greater value[89]. Moreover the development of the tea industry and the growing importance of Darjeeling as a sanatorium made it a tract of great value to the Government (ibid: 45-6).

The Government of India accepted the proposal of the Lieutenant-Governor and increased the Maharajah's allowance from Rs. 9,000 to Rs. 12,000 a year with effect from the year 1873. But in increasing the allowance the Government of India made it clear that the grant was made without any reference to the increased value of Darjeeling, but purely as a mark of consideration for the Maharajah and as an indication of the desire of the Government to

---

[88] This was the first time a Sikkim Maharajah ever visited the British territory although they were invited so many times before.

[89] From Darjeeling and the Morang alone the Government was deriving annually rents of Rs. 17,946 and Rs. 59,747 respectively (Rao 1972: 46).

assist him in improving his country and developing trade (ibid: 46). The loss of Darjeeling and Morang was the lack of diplomatic manoeuvres on the part of Maharajah of Sikkim. They were not attuned to deal diplomatically with the power like British Empire, lack in both size and capacity to deal with power like Britain, the only power Sikkim had was Tibet. Tibet also was not at par the power of British Government, and also, it was under the suzerainty of China.

The British Military Expedition to Sikkim was an unqualified success. The power of the Maharajah was considerably reduced and he had to accept all the demands put forth by the British. Under Articles 8 to 12 of the Treaty of 1861, the Government gained many trade privileges. Ashley Eden expressed the hope that a great trade would develop between Bengal and Tibet via Sikkim (ibid).

After the death of Sidkeong Namgyal in April 1874 his half-brother Thotub Namgyal was made Chogyal (Kotturan 1983: 68). After the death of Tsugphud Namgyal, his fifth wife, Rani Menchi was married to Changzed Karpo, his illegitimate son. The son by this marriage, Thinley Namgyal was considered a member of the royal family fit for succession. Thotub Namgyal had hare-lip and was considered as a sign of weak intelligence by the Sikkimese. But the British heavily came in favour of Thutob Namgyal. Edgar[90] thought that Thinley's succession would endanger the British interests as it was confirmed that he would come under the influence of ex-Dewan Namgyal who was an enemy of the British. The paramount power's choice prevailed. Thutob Namgyal was consecrated as King

---

[90] Soon after the treaty of Tumlong, Dr. Campbell was replaced by J. W. Edgar as the Deputy Commissioner of Darjeeling.

in 1874 (ibid: 70-1). H. H. Risley, who afterwards became the secretary to the Government of India commented with satisfaction "Not a whisper was heard on the frontier of the remonstrance against this vigorous piece of king-making, and Tibet acquiesced silently in an act which struck at the roots of any claim on her part to exercise a paramount influence in the affairs of the Sikkim state" (Risley 1894/1989: VI).

The increased British influence in Sikkim made the pro-Tibetan party uneasy. Edgar, who had been deputed to investigate the possibility of establishing British trade with Tibet, brought to the notice of Bengal administration; a communication addressed by the Chinese Amban in Lhasa to the ruler of Sikkim, calling upon him not to encourage road building in his territory and to prevent British officers from crossing the border into Tibet (Grover 1974: 22). They were warned that the purpose of the road building was not only for the trade, it was for the military purpose also. In case of British had to send an expedition to Tibet or in case of British had to deal with the Russian influence in Tibet, the road would serve a great purpose. Although, the call of China, not to let enter the British into Sikkimese territory or not to allow the construction of road in Sikkimese territory, were grave provocations but the British decided to overlook them and a road was constructed through Sikkim to the Jelep La on the Tibet frontier (ibid).

Thotub Namgyal, who had arisen to power with British support, could not stand up to the pressure of the anti-British Bhutiyas and Tibetans. He drifted away from the British influence and succumbed to pressure of the anti-British Bhutiyas and Tibetans. Early in 1886, he abruptly disavowed his subordination to the Government of India, as enjoined by the treaty of 1861 (ibid). It led to the skirmishes between British and Tibet in 1888, which has been already discussed in the previous chapter. It took place because of the reason that Macaulay Mission had organised under the leadership of Colman Macaulay to open up Tibet for the trade purpose and as soon as Tibet came to know about it, they assemble their troops on the frontier of Tibet and Sikkim to prevent the mission. As Viceroy was busy dealing the affairs of Burma with China, decided to abandon the mission. But Tibet did not disperse their troops and instead advanced 12 miles inside Sikkim and occupied a place called Lingtu on Darjeeling road. The reluctance of Tibetans to withdraw culminated into a full scale war and Tibetans had to suffer considerable blow from the British military[91]. After the clash with Tibetans in 1888, Anglo-Sikkimese relations entered another phase.

The Fifth Phase of Anglo-Sikkimese Relationship (1889-1914)

The fifth phase of Anglo-Sikkimese relationship enters with the creation of Political Office in Sikkim in 1889 with John Claude White as the first Political Officer of Sikkim. The charge of the Deputy Commissioner of Darjeeling with regard to Sikkim was transferred directly to the Political Officer in Sikkim[92]. By the time when Thotub Namgyal returned from exile, he met with the Council, where Claude White was the Chairman, Phodang Lama, Khangsa Dewan and the Shew Dewan were members (Namgyal 1908: 100). A

---

[91] Lingtu affairs is discussed in the preceding chapter.
[92] Political Office in Sikkim was responsible for the British relations with Tibet and Bhutan.

rudimentary administration was created to assist Maharajah in governing the state. White[93] reorganised the entire system of administration in Sikkim. He conducted land and mineral surveys and developed unoccupied waste land including the land occupied by the monasteries (Grover 1974: 24).

Claude White brought a new face to the administration of the Kingdom by modifying the land tenure system, establishment of forest department and stopped the reckless destruction of valuable sal forests in South Sikkim and established tea gardens across the border for curing of tea leaves. He also established the police department with its first police post at Aritar. He also introduced apples from England in Lachung and Lachen in North Sikkim (Pradhan 2011/2013: 220).

The unfriendly note with White in the beginning of the relationship with Maharajah turned into very cordial in a course of time. As Maharani in a private interview with Lady Minto said, "..... Mr. White, Political Officer in Sikkim taught us how to collect rents, and taxes, to administer justice, and in every way improved the condition of Sikkim and shed the light of knowledge in the benighted little State" (Namgyal 1908: 140-41). In the time of White, Sikkim for the very first time witnessed how a modern state system works and the things were introduced to modernise the state.

After White, Charles Bell became the Political Officer of Sikkim[94]. In the long array of British Political Officers, Bell was the only officer of the Raj who knew in totality the 'Tibetan

---

[93] White was an officer in the Public Works Department of British Government.

[94] He was a diplomat par excellence and his Tibet Policy was followed throughout by all his successors till the independence of India.

mentality' and the Dalai Lama's Court had the highest regard and full trust in him (Pradhan ibid: 220-21). By 1908, the British Government had consolidated its position over Sikkim to such an extent that Government of India experienced no trouble either from the Maharajah or from the outside powers like Tibet and China. In 1914, after the death of Maharajah Thotub Namgyal, Sidkeong Namgyal became the Maharajah, ignoring the claims of his elder brother Tchoda Namgyal[95], but he was not destined to rule for a long time. He died on 5th December 1914 and he was succeeded by his younger brother, Tashi Namgyal (Rao 1972: 145).

It is evident from the above discussions that, within a decade of the establishment of Political Office in Sikkim, the Government of India consolidated its authority in Sikkim to such an extent that it was able to meddle with liberty in important affairs concerning the royal family. The silent assent of the royal family and the people in the decisions of the Government of India indicated the nature and extent of British authority in Sikkim (ibid: 123).

The Sixth Phase of Anglo-Sikkimese Relationship (1914-1947)

With the accession of Tashi Namgyal to the throne of Sikkim, the British relations with Sikkim entered into another happy

---

95 By the refusal of Tchoda Namgyal to return to Sikkim, Government of India decided that, by his own act he surrendered his claim to the succession. Government of British India, therefore, in February 1899 recognised Sidkeong Namgyal as the successor-designate to the Sikkim throne. At the same time Tchoda Namgyal was prohibited from entering into Sikkim.

phase. The Maharajah was under the tutelage of Sir Charles Bell, then Political Officer (Grover 1974: 28). Maharajah remained a loyal friend of the British till the end of their rule in India. The Government of India was so much satisfied with his loyalty that it restored to him the powers over the internal administration of the Kingdom (Rao 1972: 145). The documents in Sikkim Archives tell us how cordial the relation was under the reign of Tashi Namgyal. As per the document No.777/E, dated, 27th March 1916[96], the Government of India had directed Political Officer to give the control of the departments, namely; Excise, Income tax, Police, Jail and Judicial and Revenue Stamps to the King. It shows the trust of the Government of India on Maharajah that the Government agreed to transfer the full powers to Maharajah over the internal administration of Sikkim.

Another instance is when Triple Entente was victorious over the Triple Alliance in the First World War. The Government of India referred a letter to His Highness Maharajah, to share the happiness of the victory over Axis power on 9th July 1919, which read as:

> "The Government of India have suggested to Local Government that the 19th July should be notified as a public holiday, this being the date fixed for the Peace Celebrations in England. As the hot weather is unsuitable for celebrations in India the general celebrations will take place in India next cold weather but it is thought that the actual signing of the

[96] This is a letter from C. A. Bell to His Highness the Maharajah of Sikkim (See Annexure: X).

peace treaty should not pass unnoticed in India. The Public holiday on the 19th July is therefore being arranged and I am notifying it for my own offices and subordinate offices. Flags will be flown and such other methods adopted as may be suitable to indicate that the day is one of public rejoicing. The Government of India have suggested to Local Governments the advisability of arranging at all principal centres throughout each province of all officials and as many as possible of the non-official population to whom the peace terms in connection with Germany would be publicly summarized by the head of the district or other chief local civil authority. I should like to arrange that any non-officials who care to do so may be present at the meeting which I propose to hold for Government servants on the 19th July as the Government of India think it desirable that the nature of the peace terms imposed on Germany should be made known as widely as possible.

The weather makes it unlikely that an outdoor meeting can be arranged and so I propose to hold the meeting in one of the vacant barracks as being perhaps the largest room available. I shall be grateful for Your Highness's cooperation in letting the general public know that the meeting is open to all and hope to have an opportunity of discussing details at an early date"[97].

In a response to this, the Maharajah orders in a document No.919/G.B.[98]that special prayers in all monasteries in Sikkim should be repeated for three days and that the coming years may be of peace, happy and prosperity. In another letter to the Maharajah from the Viceroy of India, invites Maharajah to take part in the Chamber of Princes[99] and in other ceremonies, dated 22nd November 1920, in which Field Marshall the Duke of Connaught had come on behalf of King Emperor of Britain, to inaugurate the Chamber of Princes. It shows the cordial ties between British Government and Sikkim after 1914. In a reply to this, Maharajah Tashi Namgyal says, dated 9th October, 1920; "My friend, I send you, for your information, a post copy of my telegram of today's date respecting my going to Delhi to attend the inauguration ceremony of the Chamber of Princes"[100].

Another exchange of letters which shows the cordial ties between Sikkim and British Government is, on the occasion of hostility of Amir of Afghanistan towards India, the letter sent by Viceroy and Governor-General read as:

> "I greatly regret to inform Your Highness that the Amir Amanulla has, without warning and without provocation, moved troops to the Indian frontier and has committed acts of

---

[97] See Annexure: XI
[98] See Annexure: XII
[99] See Annexure: XIII
[100] See Annexure: XIV

hostility which render collision between our forces and those of Afghanistan"[101].

In a reply to this, the Maharajah writes to Viceroy of India;

"I beg to acknowledge the receipt of Your Excellency's favour of the 9th May 1919 and to express my surprise at hearing of the audacity shown in the unprovoked act of hostility on the part of the Amir of Afghanistan. I however feel quite sure that he will soon be brought to his senses and compelled to see the folly of the step he has presumed to take against the Indian Government. I beg to assure Your Excellency of the firm faith and loyalty of my little State and of my own sincere allegiance to the King Emperor and my readiness to do my best. The number of Muslim subjects in my little State is so small that I am sure to be able to prevent them from creating any trouble"[102].

From the above account it is clear that Maharajah's submission to British Government led to the cordial relation between Sikkim and India. It lasted till the end of British rule in India. After the independence of India, the relation entered into a different phase, demands raised for the democratisation of Sikkim and political transformation.

---

[101] See Annexure: XV
[102] See Annexure: XVI

Conclusion

It is clear from the above facts that the relation had been uneven between the British and Sikkim. Since the beginning of the relationship, Sikkim began to lose its sovereignty and autonomy. British Government did not miss any chance to play a bargaining card to attach a possession of Sikkim, even though the British Government did return some of the lost territories of Sikkim in Gorkha-Sikkim war (1788-92), gained through the treaty of Sugauli in 1815 with Nepal. But the reason behind returning some of these territories was to build Sikkim as a string buffer state with regard to Nepal, Bhutan and Tibet/China. The British presence in Sikkim did not allow Nepal and Bhutan to come into direct contact with each other. In the past they were involved in several skirmishes and as a result of that Sikkim had to lose some of its territories.

Sikkim stands in between with Nepal in the west, Bhutan in the south-east, Tibet in the north-east and India in the south. This strategic location of Sikkim rendered a firm British presence and with British presence in Sikkim they minimised the probability of war amongst the Eastern Himalayan states and made Eastern Himalayan region stable. With British coming in contact with Sikkim, these Eastern Himalayan states never went to war again with each other, as they did before the intervention of British in the Eastern Himalayan region. British Government promoted this region into a stable zone by their influence and diplomatic tactics, to protect themselves from the powers like Tsarist Russia and China.

Three of the states had come under the influence of British Government, Tibet with the support of China and was suzerain state of China was absconding to come into the influence of British. Tibet was not obeying the clauses of the Convention signed by China on behalf of Tibet. But with the Younghusband Mission, Tibet could not avoid the British presence in Eastern Himalaya and had to succumb under the influence of British Government. The fact that Tibet was not opening up for the trade with British was, they had Lamaist tradition and felt threatened that British would make some changes on their tradition, it is said that they were more afraid of British Missionaries than British army.

Playing a bargaining card British kept relations with these states which were colonial peripheries. But India which was at the core of colonialism, they had direct kind of approach. They were subjugated directly by using military force, they changed the dynamics of the whole institution and was heavily shaped and influenced by the colonialism. The original voice of India was totally silenced by the British. But in case of colonial peripheries British had a different approach, the states were allowed to retain their autonomy in internal affairs though their foreign relations were fully controlled by Britain. Britain did not allow the Tibetan delegation to visit Beijing, but after the independence of India, India allowed the delegation to visit Beijing (Jian 2006: 59). It is evident from this, that how British had controlled the foreign affairs of these peripheral states.

CHAPTER IV

Impact of the End of British Paramountcy in South Asia on Sikkim

Sikkim's status was not defined and it was an undecided and unguaranteed state at the time of British withdrawal from India/South Asia in 1947. Sikkim had deep political relations with Great Britain for almost 130 years and the British had been playing a decisive role in the affairs of Sikkim throughout this period. Sikkim politics was largely shaped and influenced by the British interests in the region which has been discussed in the preceding chapters. The 130 years old relation between Sikkim and Great Britain came to an end on the eve of India's independence. Sikkim had enjoyed a unique position under British Imperial Raj[103]. Great Britain pulled her hands in guaranteeing the position of Sikkim, in the changed situation[104]. Because of its strategic location,

---

[103] Sikkim was never a feudatory native state in the precise meaning of that term as it was understood in the British India. But in practice neither was it independent nor even autonomous internally during the British period. A unique combination of circumstances centering around the efforts to protect India's north-eastern frontiers and to open Tibet in the latter decades of the nineteenth century, finally led the British to establish a formal "Protectorate" over Sikkim (Grover 1974: 85).

[104] The Memorandum of the cabinet mission and the Viceroy dated

Sikkim was accorded with special status in its relations with independent India somewhat similar to the Princely States[105] (Kotturan 1983: 93, Grover 1974: 86). After the termination of British paramountcy in India, all the treaties signed between British Government, Princely States and Eastern Himalayan states became null and void. The question of the inheritance of the relations by independent India with regard to Princely States and other Eastern Himalayan states in general and Sikkim in particular is the focus of this chapter. This Chapter critically examines the issues related to the transfer of authority from Colonial Crown to India.

As British pulled itself out of India, the question of continuance of relations between Great Britain, Princely States and Eastern Himalayan states did not arise. The British imperial interest in the region became a question of less relevance. In this context, independent India was at the core of the future relations. India took over the relations from British Government, which the Princely States and Eastern Himalayan states had had with the British. Resultantly, Indian interests became the deciding factor in the future relations of these states.

---

16 May, 1946 said: "Before putting forward our recommendation we turn to deal with the relationship of the Indian states to British India. It is quite clear that with the attainment of independence by British India, whether inside or outside the British Commonwealth, the relationship which has hitherto existed between the Rulers of the states and the British Crown will no longer be possible. Paramountcy can neither be retained by the British Crown nor transferred to the new Government" (Grover 1974: 83).

[105] Unconsciously Nehru's inheritance of the British psychology of buffer zones to secure India's northern frontiers, helped Sikkim in achieving a separate special status (Grover 1974: 94).

In 1941, when the reorganisation of the old Political Department of the Government of India took place, it was decided to leave Sikkim affairs in the hands of the Political Department. In 1945 the question came up again as to whether it was appropriate for the External Affairs Department to deal with Sikkim. There were two schools of thought in the India Office; one suggested that as a frontier state, 'Sikkim is important because of its connections with Tibet, it should be the concern of the External Department, rather as Baluchistan and the North-West Frontier were'. The other school found no reason why the internal affairs of Sikkim should be handled by the External Department, particularly since the state's affairs were no longer affected by Tibet. Finally, it was decided that the Political Officer or Resident should continue to address the Political Department in India[106] (Singh 1988: 254).

In 1935, a new constitution for India was enacted. A. K. J. Singh (1988: 257) says "The Government of India Act of 1935 bound Sikkim to the Constitution of India as an Indian State". In case of Sikkim, Political Officer was in charge of Sikkim's external relation with the Indian Government. Just before the enactment of 1935 Act, Maharaj Kumar Palden Thondup Namgyal led official delegation went to Delhi for discussions with the Chamber of Princes, a body representing the Princely States of India in their relations with the Government of India. Sikkim's strategic position, bounded on three sides by foreign territory and only one side by British India, had been acknowledged in the various

---

[106] IOR: *L/P&S/13/1499*, IO minutes, 20-24 Oct 1945 (Singh 1988: 285).

treaties that the British had negotiated with the state. The 1935 Act also recognised this special position and the Political Officers were permitted to continue to conduct Sikkim's political relations (ibid: 257-58).

In reality, Act of 1935 did not bind Sikkim to Indian Constitution, and Sikkim did not become a princely state of India. However, the name of Sikkim appeared in the list of "Indian States" which is according to the Act of 1935, 'any territory whether described as a State, an Estate, a jagir or otherwise, belonging to or under the suzerainty of a Ruler who is under the suzerainty of British Empire and not being part of British India' (Act of 1935: 199). But, there was a provision that states under Indian State could become a part of Indian federation if only the ruler of a state in negotiation with Governor General accedes his/her state to Indian federation (ibid: 84), which Sikkim never did. Surjit Mansingh in *India's Search for Power: Indira Gandhi's Foreign Policy 1966-1982 (1984: 280)* says, "It (Sikkim) was listed as an Indian Princely State in the India Act of 1935 which provided a new constitution for the subcontinent". However, the fact of the matter is that, though the 'Act of 1935' did provide a new constitution for India, it did not list Sikkim as an Indian Princely State, there is no such term as – princely state – in the Act of 1935. By virtue of Instrument of Accession, it was not acceded to India due to its special position which even the Act of 1935 recognised. The status of Sikkim remained unchanged, it remained as it was before the Act of 1935.

In short, even after the enforcement of the Act, Sikkim remained in the hands of Political Department and Secretary of State was the head of the matters related to Sikkim. As per the Government of India Act 1935, "The Secretary of State shall lay before Parliament the draft of any Instrument of Instructions (including any Instrument amending or revoking an Instrument previously issued) which it is proposed to recommend His Majesty to issue to the Governor-General, and no further proceedings shall be taken in relation thereto except in pursuance of an address presented to His Majesty by both Houses of Parliament praying that the Instrument may be issued" (ibid: 9). Secretary of State had the power to present any instructions before the Parliament, even to revoke the instructions which were previously issued, which is to be issued to the Governor General. In this regard no alternative option would be taken but to issue the instructions presented by the Secretary of State.

Office of the Secretary of State and Governor General were different and directly accountable to the British Parliament. However, as mentioned earlier, the instructions provided by Secretary of State to Parliament to issue the orders to Governor General shall not be changed and had to make arrangements to issue that order. Even after the independence of India, Political Office in Sikkim was continued under the Department of External Affairs, Government of India and it remained till 1975. If the affairs of Sikkim were dealing by External Affairs Department then there is no question about becoming Sikkim a part of India. After the independence of India, Sikkim was not acceded into the Indian Union despite the demand from the local leaders of Sikkim State Congress[107] (SSC). India could not

---

[107] A political party formed under the leadership of Tashi Tshering on 7th December 1947.

do that because India did not have the legitimate right to do that.

In May 1946, the Viceroy Lord Wavell declared that under the new constitution of India, Britain would cease to exercise the powers of paramountcy in relation to the Indian States. There was general recognition by both the Government of India and the Constituent Assembly created on 21st December 1946, which was responsible for drafting the new Constitution of India; that Sikkim was in a special category, recognition that Sikkim had a special position was accorded on 22nd January 1947 when the Constituent Assembly adopted a resolution moved by Jawaharlal Nehru, then Vice President of the Viceroy's Executive Council, that 'this Assembly resolves that the committee to confer with the negotiating committee set up by the Chamber of Princes and with other representatives of Indian States for certain specified purposes shall in addition have power to confer with such persons as the committee thinks fit for the purpose of examining the special problem of Bhutan and Sikkim and to report to the Assembly the result of such examination'. Nehru knew well that a committee set up for the purpose of discussing terms with Indian Princes would have no authority to enter into discussions with Sikkim and Bhutan. Therefore, additional power was ascribed to the committee; it was to negotiate with territories which are not Indian States, Bhutan and Sikkim, and it was to have special authority to meet representatives of Sikkim and Bhutan and discuss any special problem that may arise (Singh 1988: 260-1).

Recognising this, Maharajah Tashi Namgyal wrote to Lord Pethick Lawrence, Secretary of State for India, who had brought the Cabinet Mission to Delhi to discuss the transfer of power and setting out the problems affecting Sikkim. In his view, technically Sikkim was an Indian State as per the provisions in the Government of India Act 1935, but in reality she was not an Indian state as she had a totally different, historical, cultural and even political trajectory. He hoped that 'no decision directly affecting Sikkim will be taken without due consideration of the position of Sikkim as a border State and without giving the Sikkim representative an opportunity of setting forth the peculiarities of the case before the Cabinet Ministers'[108]. The Maharajah was assured that the *Memorandum on States' Treaties and Paramountcy*, presented by the Cabinet Delegation to the Chamber of Princes, would provide an answer to the Maharajah's questions in this regard. A. J. Hopkinson, then Political Officer of Sikkim, 'thought the Cabinet Delegation's reply was less than adequate, he pointed to the fact that the paramountcy memorandum itself did not touch on the most important and peculiar aspect of Sikkim's case, which was that the state was surrounded on three sides by foreign territory and that, in view of this peculiarity, it would require special consideration' (ibid: 261).

The India Office responses to the plea was not reassuring, they saw no alternative but for Sikkim, long established as an Indian State, to negotiate its future position with the Indian Union like any other state under paramountcy. As for the spiritual relationship of the inhabitants of Sikkim to Dalai Lama, the India Office could not see its relevance,

---

[108] IOR:L/P&S/13/1449, P. 1041, Maharaja Tashi Namgyal to Pethick-Lawrence, 10 may 1946 (Singh 1988).

since Sikkim had no political relationship with the Tibetan Government. The recognition of a small separate unit was itself problematical and especially since there was no other Indian State with which it could be unified. Added to which, independent India had still to evolve a policy towards its North-Eastern Frontier and to any complications which might arise in the region in future (ibid).

All in all, the India Office visualised the Indian Government having no alternative but to consider maintaining the northern principalities in virtual independence of India as buffer and, as far as possible, client states. 'There may be greater advantage in according Sikkim a more independent status than in seeking to absorb Sikkim and Bhutan in the Indian Union'[109]. There was some doubt in the India Office whether the special conditions attached to Sikkim could be realistically or practically recognised by the Indian Union. Before the transfer of power, the Maharajah, having received no further assurances regarding Sikkim's position in relation to the Indian Union, wrote to Lord Louis Mountbatten, then Viceroy and submitted a memorandum with questions on the status of his state (ibid: 260).

On 25th July 1947, Lord Louis Mountbatten had a meeting with all the Princes of India. As a result of this meeting, A. J. Hopkinson was instructed to inform the Maharajah that, in the interests of India and Sikkim, the existing posts concerned with Sikkim's political relations would continue to be maintained under the control of the External Affairs Department in Delhi (ibid: 261).

---

[109] ibid, Minute by Patrick, 10 Aug 1946 (Singh 1988).

Accordingly Hopkinson wrote to Maharajah on 26th July 1947:

> I have the honour to say that the government of India have come to the conclusion that it would be in the interest of both the dominion of India and Sikkim, Tibet and Bhutan that existing posts concerned with their political relations should continue to be maintained under the dominion government acting through the Department of External Affairs.

> The government of India recognize Sikkim's special position: the presence of an officer at Gangtok simultaneously responsible for relations with Sikkim, Tibet and Bhutan, it may be observed, is the best possible guarantee of this fact. The government of India trust that in the circumstances the durbar will agree to the continuance of a post equivalent to that of Political Officer, the incumbent of that post having supervision over posts in Tibet.

> The government of India add that this proposal in no way modifies the position as understood in the recent conversations with representatives of the durbar at New Delhi (Datta-Ray 1984/2004: 49-50).

It was pointed out that the presence of an officer at Gangtok, simultaneously responsible for relations with Sikkim, Tibet and Bhutan, was the best guarantee for the

Kingdom's special position to continue to be recognised. The Indian Government hoped, in that circumstances, the Sikkim authorities would agree to the continuance of a post equivalent to that of Political Officer who would have overall supervision of posts in Tibet as well (Singh 1988: 257). On 1st April 1948 the Durbar agreed to the proposal for the continuance of the post of a representative of the External Affairs Ministry at Gangtok, and also for the conduct of relations with Tibet and having supervision over posts in Tibet (Datta-Ray 1984/2004: 50-1). The intention was to maintain the post permanently, and in consequence the other subordinate and ministerial staffs were also to be retained (Singh 1988: 257).

The Relationship of Sikkim with Independent India

The Maharajah, Barmiok Athing-la and Roop Narayan, an Indian judge who served Sikkim for about 20 years, decided to explore the interest of New Delhi. But the meeting with Sir Brojendra Lal Mitter, Dewan of Baroda, was not successful. Mitter advised the Sikkimese to "close your eyes and jump into the ocean of India", to which Athing-la retorted: "Your freedom is not necessarily mine. If independence comes to India it should also come to Sikkim". The meetings with Maulana Azad and Dr. Rajendra Prasad were equally unfruitful, as they knew nothing about Sikkim and had no clear idea of the future (Datta-Ray 1984/2004: 47-8).

Sir Edward Wakefield of the Political Department was more understanding. The delegation asked a number of pertinent questions when they called on him on 15th June 1946 and insisted on being kept informed of the exact nature of India's ties with Tibet, Nepal and Bhutan. Wakefield assured the visitors that "it should be possible for Sikkim to obtain nearly identical terms of political relationships with India as Bhutan and Nepal obtained"[110]. In his opinion, "Sikkim should not be afraid of being carried away on a flood of decisions made in regard to the Princely States" (ibid: 48).

More formal guidelines were set in the Constituent Assembly of India in this regard on 22nd January 1947. Nehru knew that the Narendra Mahal team[111] could not speak for the two Himalayan kingdoms and additional power was ascribed, as mentioned before briefly. There were more conferences that year. At a crucial meeting on 16th July, the three Sikkim delegates met V.P. Menon, Sir Humphrey Trevelyan, and Harishwar Dayal of the States and External Affairs Departments. Roop Narayan argued that Sikkim's geopolitical location and ethnic and cultural affinities called for parity with Bhutan. Menon admitted that Maharajah Tashi Namgyal's status was different from any other ruler of Princely States and that Sikkim was under no obligations to join India. Menon did, however, express the wish that the Durbar would not sever all connections with India. He suggested that even without accession, Sikkim and Bhutan could enter into agreements with independent India on defence, external affairs, and communications. He also

---

[110] The Indo-Bhutanese Treaty and Indo-Nepalese Treaty were already signed; fifteen months before with Bhutan and five months before with Nepal, when Sikkim's relation with India was decided (Datta-Ray, 1984/2004, p. 48).

[111] A committee set up for the express purpose of discussing terms with Indian Princes (Singh 1988: 255).

assured to the visitors that India's External Affairs Ministry would continue to handle relations with Gangtok. He further assured the delegation that the Durbar did not have to be represented on 25th July when Mountbatten discusses the future of Princely States with rulers (ibid: 49).

Political Activities in Sikkim

Like in other native states, the independence movement in India had given inspiration to similar movements in Sikkim (Kotturan 1983: 94). Political activities in Sikkim started simmering since the end of 1945 (Datta-Ray 1984/2004: 52). First it was confined to isolated pockets with social rather than political aims. The Indian independence and the establishment of popular governments in some states encouraged these organisations to come together with pronounced political aims. The aims of the movements were to overthrow Bhutia-Lepcha elites control in general and the authority of Kazis in particular. They also aimed at destroying the power of Thekedars[112] (ibid). On 7th December 1947, the leaders of these regional organisations[113] met at Gangtok and called for a political awakening in Sikkim. In a largely attended public meeting at Gangtok, a new political party, the Sikkim State Congress[114] was formed with Tashi Tshering

---

[112] Nepalese lessee-landowners.

[113] At the capital, Gangtok, there was Praja Sudharak Samaj under the leadership of Tashi Tshering, Praja Sammelan under the leadership of Gobardhan Pradhan at Temi Tarku of South Sikkim and Praja Mandal at Chakhung, West Sikkim, under the leadership of Kazi Lhendup Dorji Khangsarpa (Kotturan 1983: 94).

[114] In an interview with Mr. C. D. Rai on 29th December 2013, he was

as its President. It is important to note here that similar political parties had been in existence in other princely states and some of them were already in power (Kotturan 1983: 94-5).

The formation of the Sikkim State Congress was a landmark in the political history of Sikkim (ibid: 95). Mr. C. D. Rai says, "The birth of Sikkim State Congress on 7th December, 1947 can be considered as the first cockcrow of the political movement in Sikkim and it was the direct result of Indian independence on 15th August, 1947" (Rai 2011/2013: 101). With the formation of the party, a resolution was also introduced for political and economic reforms. A five member delegation went to meet the then Maharajah, Sir Tashi Namgyal on 9th December[115] and presented the memorandum incorporating the three demands formulated at the meeting of 8th December (ibid: 102). These three demands were; i) Abolition of landlordism, ii) Formation of an interim government as a precursor for a democratic form of government, and iii) the accession of Sikkim to the Union of India (Kotturan 1983: 95, Rai 2011/2013: 103).

---

the General Secretary of Sikkim State Congress. He said the Sikkim State Congress was created in the same line how the Mysore State Congress, Hyderabad State Congress were created.

[115] Mr. C. D. Rai while narrating the event said; 'when they went to present the memorandum. Tashi Tshering had written a draft about ill-treatment of Kazis and Thekedars in Sikkim and that draft became the memorandum of Sikkim State Congress. When they went to present memorandum to Maharaja, the three demands were not there, it was a plain memorandum without demands. When it was decided that there should be demands, the three demands were incorporated'.

The popular resentment culminated in the formation of Sikkim State Congress. The reason behind putting forth these demands were, regarding the first demand that is abolition of landlordism, people in Sikkim were highly oppressed by the authority of Kazis and Thekedars. Kazis and Thekedars used to collect revenues sometimes in their own account by forcing people to pay high revenues. A small amount of revenue used to go to the State treasury. To get rid of this oppression SSC put forward this demand. As per the second demand, they wanted participation of people in the State affairs. And they believed that these goals would only be achieved if Sikkim is acceded to the Union of India. They firmly pressed for this demand because by then India was already world's largest democracy.

The demands were reportedly discussed by the Maharaj Kumar Palden Thondup Namgyal[116] with his Advisors. After thorough discussions, Maharaj Kumar raised serious objections to the vital issue of Sikkim's accession to India. However, he was ready to negotiate on the other two demands. Meanwhile, the Sikkim Durbar wanted to evolve a consensus on the accession issue, and invited three Congress representatives to serve in the Government as Secretaries. The offer of the Sikkim Durbar was discussed at an emergency meeting of the Congress, and after heated arguments on the desirability of joining the Government, the Congress nominated three representatives - Sonam Tshering, Captain Dimik Singh Lepcha and Raghubir Singh Basnet, and they began to serve in the Government as Secretaries in

---

[116] Younger son of Sir Tashi Namgyal and was a crowned prince. He was declared crown prince after the death of his elder brother, Palzor Namgyal.

charge of some departments as Congress representatives (Rai 2011/2013: 103).

In order to counter the upcoming democratic agitation, and to emphasize the communal and racial differences of the Kingdom's population, Maharajah sponsored a new party called the Sikkim National Party (SNP) which was composed of mainly of the minority ethnic communities of the Lepchas and Bhutias (Rao 1972: 148). On 30th April 1948, the party passed a resolution stating that "Sikkim shall not under any circumstances accede to the dominion of India." Further it demanded a revision of "Sikkim's political relations with the Indian Union on the basis of equality" and declared that Sikkim was closer to Tibet than to India on the following grounds:

> "(a) Historically, socially, culturally and linguistically, Sikkim has closer affinities with Bhutan and Tibet.
>
> (b) From the geographical and ethnic point of view, Sikkim is not a part of India. She has only political relations with the latter which were imposed on her.
>
> (c) From the religious point of view, being a lamaist, she is quite distinct from India" (Grover 1974: 88).

The resolution declared that the policy of the party was "by all means to maintain intact the indigenous character of Sikkim and to preserve its integrity". The resolution further declared that the party would make all efforts to see that

Sikkim remained outside the Indian Union. The resolution pleaded that any attempt to force Sikkim to accede to the Indian Union, either by direct or indirect means, would be unfair because it would be a denial to Sikkim of its right to stick to its national affinities. The resolution concluded with the following appeal and a warning to India, quoting Sir Charles Bell:

> "From India's point of view, a happy Sikkim as a buffer state would be of great advantage than an unhappy Sikkim in India on one of her future international boundaries of great importance, which would be disadvantage, indeed a danger to India" (Rao 1972: 148-9, Grover 1974: 89).

To avoid any controversy and ill-feeling with the Sikkim Durbar over the questions whether Sikkim was a princely state and whether the Government of India automatically inherited the paramount rights the British had enjoyed in the border states, "standstill Agreement"[117] between the Sikkim Durbar and the Government of India was concluded and signed on February 27, 1948. This agreement stipulated that "all agreements, relations and administrative arrangements as to matters of common concern existing between the Crown

---

[117] The Indian authorities had first submitted "the Instrument of Accession" which was used for signing by the rulers of the Indian princely states on their merger into the Indian Union. When Sikkim objected to this format, India agreed to use the terminology of "Standstill Agreement", which had been suggested by the Sikkimese (Grover 1974: 87).

and the Sikkim State on August 14, 1947 were deemed to continue between the Dominion of India and the Sikkim Durbar pending the conclusion of a new agreement or treaty". This constituted an implicit recognition by India of Sikkim's special status, as well as providing an early but clear indication that the independent India would not insist upon Sikkim's complete merger with the Indian Union like other states. While replying to the question in the Constituent Assembly, B. V. Keskar, Deputy Minister of External Affairs and Commonwealth Relations said: "with regard to Sikkim, in many matters it is controlled by the Government of India but in many matters it stands independently, not exactly as a state within India. It is something between a state in India and an independent state". Prime Minister Nehru also during the course of Debate said:

> "Sikkim has not acceded. The question in that shape has not arisen. All these matters are pending and under consideration. The present position is that the old relations of Sikkim and Bhutan with the Government of India continue. What exactly the future relation will be is a matter for consideration between Sikkim, Bhutan and the Government of India" (Grover 1974: 87-8).

Furber (1951) opines that, "Sikkim and Bhutan may be described as states protected by the Republic of India, which controls their foreign affairs. New agreements have been negotiated with each of them. The difference from the pre-1947 position is that, whereas under the British regime only Bhutan was considered as outside the international frontier of India, they are now both outside that frontier" (Furber 1951: 369). In the Act of 1935, Sikkim appeared in the list of Indian states but British did not accede Sikkim into British Empire given the geo-political location of Sikkim. Bhutan had been considered outside the British Empire by the British and which was in the reality. It was the responsibility of Political Officer in Sikkim to look after the affairs of Bhutan. But after the independence of India and with the change in the nature of the government, India treated both Sikkim and Bhutan outside the Indian Territory and granted both Sikkim and Bhutan a protectorate status.

In a State Congress meeting of June, 1948, the three Congress members serving as Secretaries in the Government pleaded, "Sikkim is now on a double-edged agreement with India and that within a specific time, if it so desired, could join India. But they further submitted that after scrutiny of all state papers, they had come to the conclusion that Sikkim should remain independent" (Rai 2011/2013: 103). Tashi Tshering, the President of SSC agreed to reconsider the accession issue, if they could show state papers within ten days. Strangely, the three Secretaries failed to produce the promised state papers (ibid).

By then, these three Secretaries had fully identified themselves with the administration and that the State Congress had started having second thoughts about their utility and called for their resignation. By giving representation on a communal basis the Maharajah and his Durbar cleverly brought about division in the ranks of the State Congress and the political movement it represented. In fact the Lepchas, and the Bhutia members of the "three secretaries of the Maharajah" refused to abide by the State Congress directive to resign (Kotturan 1983: 95). Consequently, at the general meeting of the SSC held at Namchi on the 22ⁿᵈ October, 1948, the three Secretaries were expelled from the party (Rai 2011/2013: 103). The Bhutia member Mr. Sonam Tshering was largely instrumental in forming the rival-pro Durbar political party, SNP with partisan interests and toed with the official line of the Sikkim Durbar. The declared objective of the National Party was the preservation of the status quo in internal affairs. With regard to the state's relations with India, its policy was ominous (Kotturan 1983: 96).

As per the directive of the party, the President, Tashi Tshering and General Secretary Chandra Das Rai went to Delhi and called on Prime Minister, Nehru at his official residence. Tashi Tshering, the President of SSC submitted the Congress memorandum containing the three-fold demands. After glancing through the demands, Prime Minister Nehru said, "May be there are few small landlords in Sikkim. We have big and powerful landlords. We are going to abolish landlordism in India, your landlords will also go". So far as democratic responsible government was concerned, "we will help you, for we firmly believe in democracy". But he said, "Do not press for Sikkim's accession to India. We do not want to be accused of bullying small Sikkim and forcing Sikkim to join India by using pressure tactics". And he further said; "we want to see the three Himalayan Kingdoms of Sikkim, Nepal and Bhutan to grow as our independent and friendly neighbours" (Rai 2011/2013: 103).

The possible reason of taking this position by Nehru could be, India in an initial stage did not want to be blamed by the accusation of having imperial design or imperial nature inherited from Great Britain on Sikkim or any other states. In the statement, Nehru says, "We do not want to be accused of bullying small Sikkim and forcing Sikkim to join India by using pressure tactics" shows the concern of Nehru that if India accedes Sikkim into Indian Union then international opinion would be against India and as a young nation Nehru tried to identify India as a nation which has no imperial design on any state. The image building in the international level was important and India wanted to project herself as a state which believes in mutual co-existence, peace and harmony in the world. The impact of this position of Nehru was, the third demand of the SSC was dropped and immediate actions were taken to bring in reality the first two demands.

Popular Agitation of 1949

During the annual meeting of the Congress party held at Rangpo in the first week of February, 1949, the President, Tashi Tshering presented the report of his visit to Delhi, giving a detailed account of the delegation's fruitful talks with Prime Minister Nehru, with his Deputy Minister Dr. B. V. Keskar and other Congress leaders. As advised by the Prime Minister, SSC dropped the accession issue from its manifesto. With a view to pressing for the fulfilment of the twin demands, i.e., abolition of landlordism and formation of a democratic government, the Sikkim State Congress, under the leadership of Tashi Tshering, took a first positive step towards satyagraha movement. At the Rangpo Convention, a resolution was unanimously passed calling upon the people to start 'non-rent campaign' whereby "Until the demands of the Congress would be met, the people would refuse to pay land revenue and house tax" (ibid: 104).

In order to meet the open challenge of the Congress, the Sikkim Government arrested important Congress leaders and activists on the 6th February, 1949, namely Namgyal Tshering, General Secretary C. D. Rai, Ram Prasad, Jam. Ratna Bahadur Khatri, Jam. Budhiman Rai, Ongdi Bhutia, Chanchula, Abichandra Kharel, Brihaspati Prasai, Chukchum Sangdarpa, and Katuk Lama. Meanwhile a warrant of arrest was issued against its President Tashi Tshering. But on the written advice of the Political Officer, Harishwar Dayal, ICS, the execution of the warrant was kept in abeyance. About 5,000 people came to Gangtok and held demonstration at Gangtok Bazar against the arbitrary arrest of Congress leaders. When the peaceful agitation of the Congress gained momentum with more and more satyagrahis joining the movement, the Government had to give in before the united move of the people of Sikkim. After negotiation between the President and the Sikkim Durbar on the mediation by the Political Officer, the Government agreed to release the political prisoners unconditionally (ibid).

Meanwhile, the Political Officer, Harishwar Dayal accompanied by Mrs. Dayal, visited the Gangtok jail and assured the political prisoners that they would be released soon. 'The goodwill gestures shown by the Political Officer, first to keep in abeyance the warrant of arrest of Tashi Tshering and secondly visit to Gangtok jail to enquire about the condition of the prisoners, unnerved the Sikkim Durbar' (ibid).

The implication of this development was the leaders of the Congress were released unconditionally. In order to bring about an amicable settlement, talks were held followed by frequent exchange of letters between the Congress President and the Sikkim Durbar. But as there was no sign of amicable settlement, the Congress decided to launch a second satyagraha movement. Incidentally, the satyagraha movement started on 1st May and a huge procession of the satyaagrahis went to the Palace and sat on the ground. They began to shout slogans like "Down with oppression of landlords", "Gandhiji Zindabad", "Our demands must be met" etc. (ibid: 104-6).

The ruler for his own safety had to seek protection at the residence of the Political Officer (Kotturan 1983: 97). A detachment of the Indian Army was posted at Gangtok, intervened and rescued the ruler to its protection in the Indian Residency (currently Raj Bhavan) (Grover 1974: 90). Only an Indian garrison which had been posted at Gangtok could bring the situation under control (Kotturan 1983: 97). Due to these developments and after a prolonged negotiation in the Palace between the Congress President, Maharajah Tashi Namgyal and the Political Officer, Harishwar Dayal, the Maharajah acceded to the popular demand (Grover 1974: 90) and agreed to install a five – member interim Government that would include two Durbar nominees. Thus the first popular ministry was formed on 9th May, 1949 with the Congress President Tashi Tshering as the Chief Minister and included Captain Dimik Singh Lepcha and Chandra Das Rai from Sikkim State Congress and Dorji Dahdul and Reshmi Prasad Alley as Durbar nominees (Rai 2011/2013: 106).

Soon after, there emerged troubles over the functioning of the Ministry (Kotturan 1983: 97). Even this experiment failed to contain the political unrest and tension in the Kingdom (Grover 1974: 90). The Government of India was in a delicate position. Even though its sympathies were with the State Congress, which represented the majority of the population, it was unable to advise the Maharajah to accept the popular demands otherwise it might be accused of having sinister designs on kingdom situated on a sensitive international border. The Maharajah exploited the Indian Government's dilemma and dismissed the popular ministry on 6th June 1949. The Ministry remained in office for less than one month (Rao 1972: 150). Apparently, the Maharajah was unwilling to part with any real power whereas the ministry wanted to function as a full scale government with the Maharajah remaining as a Constitutional Head (Kotturan 1983: 97). In absence of any specific delineation and demarcation of the powers of the Maharajah and the Ministry, each side started blaming each other. With such chaotic conditions, the whole administration seemed to be heading towards a total collapse (Grover 1974: 90).

The Maharajah of Sikkim wrote to the Political Officer expressing his inability to carry on the administration without the assistance of the Government of India. He requested the Political Officer to take over the administration. The Political Officer had already reported to the Government of India that the State was threatened with disorder which neither the Maharajah nor the ministry would be able to control. Balakhrishna V. Keskar visited Gangtok towards the end of May 1949 and reported to the Government of India that there was tension between the Ministry and the Maharaj Kumar and there was likelihood of bloodshed (ibid: 91) and came to the conclusion that the state needed an impartial, capable administration to restore normalcy (Kotturan 1983: 97).

The Government of India accepted the Deputy Minister's recommendations. A company of troops was sent to Gangtok on June 2nd 1949. As reported earlier, the Maharajah had already sent a letter requesting the Political Officer to take over the administration pending the appointment of a Dewan to whom the Maharajah would delegate all powers necessary for carrying on the administration until normal conditions were restored. The same day, the Political Officer sent informed that the Government of India is taking responsibility for the administration of Sikkim in the interests of law and order. Thus the administration of 'twenty-nine days ministry' had ended (Grover 1974: 91). Accordingly a senior civil servant, Mr J. S. Lall took over the administration of the state on 11th of August 1949 as Dewan (Kotturan 1983: 97).

'The Indian press denounced India's fascist policy in taking over the administration of Sikkim which they characterised as on a par with her policy towards Kashmir, Junagadh, Hyderabad and Chandernagar' (Singh 1988: 263). But the fact was that Patel and Menon had assured Maharajah that India's External Affairs Ministry (not the new ministry of states) would continue to handle relations with Gangtok. Sunanda Datta-Ray (1984) says, "Given the resolution with which Patel and Menon handled native rulers and brought Hyderabad, Kashmir, and Junagadh to heel, it is most unlikely that they were moved by altruism to spare Sikkim".

In a conversation with Mr. Shattock at the British High Commission in Delhi, Political Officer, Harishwar Dayal justified his decision to bring Indian administration into Sikkim. In his view, the state was very much of a pyramidal hierarchy ranging from the feudal landlords to the Maharajah. During the last few years, the State Congress had carried on agitations against the landlords and brought them to their knees. Seeing that the feudal machine was being rapidly undermined, the Maharaj Kumar, who in Dayal's opinion, was the real ruler of Sikkim, took up the cudgels on behalf of the landlords against the State Congress. From then on, the struggle began to be one between the State Congress and the Maharaj Kumar. This led to frequent demonstrations in Gangtok against the Maharaj Kumar, and went so far as to take place in the palace grounds itself. In these circumstances, the Indian Government had no alternative but to intervene, which they did. Dayal was insistent that the agitation itself was almost entirely amongst the Sikkimese themselves, the Napalese and Indian Marwaris having generally stayed aloof. It was not the Indian Government's intention to merge Sikkim into the neighbouring districts of Darjeeling. He envisaged that, in due course, the Dewan would be assisted by a Council of Ministers and the State would come to be ruled on the pattern of those other states which are retaining their separate entity, with the Maharajah as a constitutional figurehead (ibid).

Shattock appears to have believed that it was only when the ruling house was on the point of being overthrown, that the Indian Government had come to its rescue. The British High Commission saw no reason to protest to the Indian Government that the 1948 Standstill Agreement had been violated, and it was not that they could not justify their action simply on the statement that they could not allow disorder to prevail. In Shattock's view, the major factor which had influenced Delhi to intervene in the internal administration of the state was communist infiltration from Tibet (ibid: 263-4).

This unsettled political climate provided good ground to the Government of India to have got Sikkim merged and acceded to the Indian Union. In spite of historical precedents from the British period and unstable internal political conditions, the Government of India was prepared to grant utmost autonomy to Sikkim in exchange for recognition of her "special interests". However, India did not want to take the benefit of the unstable political climate of the Kingdom or to completely integrate Sikkim with the Indian Union (Grover 1974: 91-92).

The Government of India consequently started negotiations regarding the status of Sikkim and her future relationship with India and Sikkim Durbar in late 1949[118]. By then, China had emerged as a unified, centralized and militant regime under the control of Communists in October, 1949. Notwithstanding the physical features of India's Northern frontier, Sikkim had assumed a great importance after coming into power of the Communists in China and their subsequent occupation of Tibet. This event changed the very basis of the direction of the politics of the Himalayan States. The Government of India, during the course of negotiations, had held consultations with the

---

[118] At the time of signing the standstill agreement the understanding was that a new treaty would be signed later to settle once and for all the relations between Sikkim and India (Kotturan 1983: 97).

Maharaj Kumar of Sikkim and the representatives of the various political parties in Sikkim. In fact they were invited for discussions at New Delhi in March 1950 (ibid: 91-2). All the eyes were turned to Delhi (Kotturan 1983: 97). The discussion covered the entire field of future relations between Sikkim and India and necessary administrative arrangements within the State including the association of popular representatives in the Government of the State. Provisional agreement was reached as regard to the future relationship of Sikkim with India, between the representatives of the two countries (Grover 1974: 91).

The Shift of Authority: Sikkim as an Indian Protectorate

The Maharaj Kumar of Sikkim who was authorised by the Maharajah to participate in the discussions on his behalf took to Gangtok the terms agreed upon. During the course of discussions, it was agreed that as regard to the status of Sikkim, it will be continued as a Protectorate of India. The Government of India will continue to be responsible for its external relations, defence and communications. As regard to the internal Government, the State would continue to enjoy autonomy subject to the ultimate responsibility of the Government of India, if necessary, for the maintenance of good administration and law and order (ibid: 91-2). This treaty bound Sikkim hand to foot and India became sole arbitrator in the case of Sikkim.

The leaders of the State Congress apparently got no hearing while the negotiations for the new treaty was in progress. The Maharaj Kumar was successful in keeping them away from the sources of power in Delhi. At the conclusion of the negotiations for the leaders of the people there was only the ambiguous press note of 20th March, 1950, which read as:

> For the present an officer of the Government of India will continue to be the Dewan of the state. But the Government of India's policy is one of progressive association of the people of the state with its government, policy with which happily His Highness the Maharajah is in full agreement. It is proposed, as a first step, that an Advisory Council, representative of all the interests should be associated with the Dewan. Steps will also be taken immediately to institute a village Panchayat system on an elective basis within the state. This is an essential and effective process of education in the art of popular government and it is the intention that these Panchayats should, in due course, elect a council for the state, whose functions and area of responsibility will be progressively enlarged (Kotturan 1983: 98).

Inder Malhotra, famous journalist of that time reported on this that: "I remember going to a ramshackle old Delhi hotel, not far away from the Delhi Railway Station, to hear the veteran and venerable Tashi Tshering, then leader of Sikkim Congress, lament that the Government of India was being both pusillanimous and unfair. 'Why must it deny the people of Sikkim the fruits of independence which other Indians were going to enjoy? he asked" (ibid).

The treaty was signed on the 5th of December, 1950, at Gangtok. Accordingly, Sikkim was recognized as a "Protectorate" of Indian Union. It was allowed complete internal autonomy while external affairs with defence and communications remained in the hands of the Central Government at Delhi. There was a great disappointment in the State Congress circles when the terms of the new treaty became known. The Sikkim Congress was hoping for a full responsible government in the state as a part of the Indian Union. Their representation to the Central Government did not produce any result since Delhi was reluctant at the moment to interfere in what could have been construed as internal affairs of the state. Now the state political parties had left with no choice but to fight it out themselves with the Sikkim Durbar (ibid: 98-9).

The Treaty of 1950 marked the beginning of a new chapter in India-Sikkim relations. It contained thirteen Articles: Article I stipulated that all previous treaties between the British Government and Sikkim which are at present in force as between India and Sikkim are hereby formally cancelled; Article II confer that Sikkim will remain Protectorate of India and enjoy internal autonomy; Article III gave Government of India responsibility of the defence and territorial integrity of Sikkim, with the right to station troops anywhere within Sikkim which shall be done in consultation with Government of Sikkim. And Sikkim agreed that she will not import any arms, ammunitions, military stores or other warlike material without prior consent of the Government of India[119].

---

[119] See Annexure: XVII

Article IV cautioned Sikkim to keep any kind of relations with foreign governments and if she desires so then it shall be conducted and regulated solely by the Government of India be it political, economic or financial. And regarding subjects of Sikkim, it was decided that subjects travelling to foreign countries shall be treated as Indian protected persons for the purpose of the passports and shall receive abroad the same protection and facilities as Indian nationals receive from Indian representatives (ibid).

Despite the insistence of Sikkim State Congress, India did not accede Sikkim to Indian Union only because India would have been accused of being fascist power. India had to develop its international identity among the comity of nations and developing identity through action is the best way to build an identity and Nehru knew this well. But in spite of having not included Sikkim into Indian Union, the process of Sikkim drifting towards India had started. By providing Sikkim subjects same passports as Indian nationals and giving protection and facilities as Indian nationals received in abroad, the degradation of Sikkim as an independent state had started with 1950 Treaty.

Article V on trade issue it was decided that Sikkim shall not levy any import duty, transit duty or other tax on goods brought into or transit through Sikkim. Likewise, Government of India also agreed not to levy import or other duty on goods of Sikkimese origin, brought into India from Sikkim.

Article VI gave Government of India an exclusive right of constructing, maintaining and regulating the use of railways, aerodromes, landing grounds, air navigation facilities, posts, telegraphs, telephones and wireless installations in Sikkim, and Government of Sikkim shall render every possible assistance in the construction, maintenance and protection of the same. Government of India shall also have the right to construct and maintain roads for the strategic purposes and for the purpose of improving communications with India and other adjoining countries and the Government of Sikkim shall render every possible assistance in the construction, maintenance and protection of such roads. Government of Sikkim may construct, maintain and regulate the use of facilities to such an extent as may be agreed by Government of India (ibid).

According to Article VII, subjects of Sikkim and Indian nationals shall have the right to entry into and free movement in India as well as Sikkim. Government of Sikkim may prescribe in consultation with Government of India that Indian nationals shall have the right to carry on trade and commerce in Sikkim and when established in any trade in Sikkim, the right to acquire, hold and dispose of any property, movable or immovable, for the purposes of the trade or residence in Sikkim. Subjects of Sikkim shall have the same right in India (ibid).

Article VIII regarding law, it was agreed that Indian nationals within Sikkim shall subject to the laws of Sikkim and subjects of Sikkim within India shall subject to the laws of India. Whenever any criminal proceedings are initiated in Sikkim against any Indian national or any person in the service of the Government of India or any foreigner, the Government of Sikkim shall refer to the Representative of the Government of India in Sikkim (hereinafter referred to as the Indian Representative) with particulars of charges against such persons. If in case of any person in the service of the Government of India or any foreigner it is so demanded by the Indian Representative, such person shall be handed over to him for trial before such court as may be established for the purpose by the Government of India either in Sikkim or outside (ibid).

Article IX imply; fugitive in either Sikkim or India shall extradite to each other's jurisdiction if both the Governments agreed upon as extradition offence. Under Article X Government of India agreed to pay sum of rupees three lakhs every year so long as the terms of this Treaty are duly observed by the Government of Sikkim. Article XI gave the right to Government of India to appoint a Representative to reside in Sikkim and Government of Sikkim shall provide him and his staff with all reasonable facilities in regard to their residential and office accommodation and generally in regard to their carrying out their duties in Sikkim. Article XII said if any dispute arises in the interpretation of the provisions of this treaty which cannot be resolved by mutual consultation, the dispute shall be referred to the Chief Justice of India whose decision there on shall be final and binding to both parties. Article XIII gave this treaty shall come into force without ratification from the date of its signature by both parties (ibid).

Some observers opine that the status was accorded to Sikkim vis-à-vis the pre-1947 with British Government in India. However, by making Sikkim its protectorate, India secured for itself rights compatible with Sikkim's internal autonomy (Grover 1974: 95). When observers pointed out that status accorded to Sikkim was similar to the status under British Imperial Raj, they are right in their terms. The change of power in India and communist revolution in China did not change the geo-politics of the region. Independent India's strategic interest was similar to the British strategic interest in the region. By granting Sikkim a protectorate status India had effectively secured the frontier defences.

The treaty signalled a close and fraternal relationship between the two people. It was hailed both in India and Sikkim as binding. It led Sikkim and India into an eternal and everlasting friendship and mutual cooperation. In India, the treaty was hailed as a big step in strengthening the frontier defence of India. The treaty reflected clearly India's heightened concern with her frontier security. The Hindustan Times dated December 7, 1950 commented:

> "This treaty will be hailed as a big step in strengthening frontier defences. Now that the Himalayas are no longer insuperable barriers as of old, it is a matter of vital import to ensure adequate safeguards along the frontiers" (ibid: 95-6).

For Sikkim, the treaty confirmed the irrelevance of the idea of an "isolationist policy" which could no longer be considered feasible, on account of the deep inroads of Indian nationalist and democratic ideals had made into the value systems of Sikkimese elite and the re-emergence of China as an expansionist and revolutionary power interested in inter-Himalayan politics. Although Sikkim had come under the protection of India, its distinct personality, traditions, customs and beliefs have in no way been jeopardised by the treaty. Having aligned itself with India, the treaty ensured Sikkim's emergence into modern world through

Indian aid and assistance. Virtually the entire development budget is met by India through direct grants-in aid, loans or subsidies. Since the conclusion of the treaty in 1950, substantial financial aid had been given and the Indian tap of cooperation remained open all the time (ibid: 96).

The treaty gave shape and substance to the broad understanding and friendship that existed between India and Sikkim for the last many decades. Therefore, it was hailed as a happy document. In his first ever interview given to the Press correspondents then touring with Prime Minister of India, during Nehru's visit to Sikkim in 1952, the Maharajah of Sikkim, Tashi Namgyal said:

> "Sikkim had confidence and trust in India and that mutual confidence between the two countries would give no cause for regret for the close relationship brought about by the 1950 Treaty" (ibid).

But the major political party of the Kingdom, SSC, was greatly disappointed with the Treaty since it wanted Sikkim to be merged with India (ibid). It is evident that the members of SSC representing the people's aspiration, for the first time, demanded for the merger with India. Government of India rejected this option and instead signed an agreement with Sikkim making Sikkim her protectorate.

Thus the India-Sikkim Treaty of 1950 disappointed both the pro-Tibetans, who wanted Sikkim to become independent with complete sovereign status on the one hand and pro-Indians, who wanted Sikkim's full accession to India in the interests of her democratic development, on the other. The former were unhappy over its status as Protectorate and the leaders of State Congress were also unhappy that India favoured the ruler against the democratic aspirations of the people. They contended that monarchy had been saved due to the strength adduced to it by India and the Indian Army. In preserving the status-quo, India appeased the pro-Tibetan minority in power in Sikkim at the cost of alienating the vast majority of population. Even in 1954, the State Congress had sent a deputation to wait on Nehru demanding their representation on "a Parliament which controls their external affairs, defence and communications", but without any success (ibid: 96-7).

The major implication of this treaty on Sikkim was that the Durbar got what it wanted; internal autonomy with the secured borders. The only resentment was mainly felt around the circles of SSC. After the signing of the treaty, political activities in Sikkim became more intense. There were frequent quarrel between the Maharaj Kumar and Congress leaders. With more political parties coming to the scene, Sikkim became the ground for political activities, which ultimately culminated into mass protest and the traditional structure of Government was changing due to people coming to power.

However, the critics say that "Articles 3,4,5,6 and 12 of the Treaty seem to render Sikkim a sui generis dependency of India... In making Sikkim one of her dependencies, occupied the old strategic position gained more than sixty years ago by British India, enabling her to guard all the Himalayan passes in the region of Kalimpong and Gangtok, north east of Darjeeling" (ibid: 97).

Neville Maxwell contends that in the case of Sikkim, India, in 1949, seized the opportunity of a local uprising against the ruler to send troops, and bring the state into closer dependence as a protectorate than it had formally been under the British. It was also contended that a "Protectorate" is more consonant with the nineteenth century concepts of international relations than the contemporary world. The India-Sikkim Treaty, therefore, according to critics, was in no way different from the treaties concluded between the British and the Indian rulers. Thus "the treaty of 1950 has robbed Sikkim of all external sovereignty and to uphold the sanctity of the internal sovereignty is mere window-dressing. Both external and internal sovereignty are complementary to one another; one cannot be separated from the other" (ibid). The critic further says: "therefore, to hail the Indo-Sikkim treaty as one of equality and mutual benefit is merely to clothe the true nature of the treaty, which so intimately binds Sikkim hand and foot to India, is a subsidiary treaty, designed to degrade Sikkim into the Indian Union in a true imperialistic manner" (ibid).

In the opinion of Chief Justice Hidayatullah of the Indian Supreme Court, the Treaty (1950) was unequal to say the least. He cited nine clauses which pointed to the true indication of Sikkim's sovereign status. The use of the term treaty, the fact that India and Sikkim were named as consenting states in the preamble, the Indian Government's appointment of a plenipotentiary, the need for the Maharajah to examine and accept Harishwar Dayal's credentials, the cancellation of earlier treaties, the use of customary legal language, the extradition clause, the appointment of an Indian representative in Gangtok, and finally the provision for ratification of the treaty (Singh 1988: 261). Hidayatullah argued that India's claim to sovereignty could not be justified in view of the fact that the treaty itself was proof that a sovereign Kingdom had voluntarily agreed to entrust some of its administrative functions to the Government of India. Nor could India put forward previous claims, based on earlier conventions, since Article I of the 1950 Treaty explicitly stated that "all previous treaties between the British Government and Sikkim had been formally cancelled". In fact, if Sikkim had been recognised, as Sir Olaf Caroe, Indian Foreign Secretary, had suggested in 1947 as a dependency of India, then the 1950 Treaty could not be considered because, unless each contracting party has a distinct sovereign international personality (ibid).

The India Office viewed the sequence of events with considerable suspicion. One view was that the Indian Government had classed Sikkim with Nepal as an area of communist activity, since the Indian Congress had never been strong in Sikkim they had decided to use the State Congress as an instrument to gain their influence in the state. Sir Algernon Rumbold's[120] opinion was somewhat different. Sikkim had not acceded to India and, therefore, the action of the Indian Government was a considerable extension of the 'theory of intervention' which they had developed already in relation to other acceding States'. 'In so far as they take their stand on the Standstill Agreement, it is relevant that Kashmir had a Standstill Agreement with Pakistan, but not with India. Consequently, if the Standstill Agreement gives India a right to intervene in Sikkim, Pakistan would have

---

[120] Assistant Secretary at India Office. Retrieved on 27/02/2014, url: (www.indpendent.co.uk/news/people/obituary-sir-algernon-rumbold-1465721.html)

a right to intervene in Kashmir'. The logic of Rumbold's argument was legally irrefutable (ibid).

As pointed out by Hidayatullah, if sovereignty of Sikkim was not violated then argument put forward by Neville Maxwell seems logical that internal and external sovereignty are complementary to each other and one cannot survive in absence of another. If India contended that the treaty (1950) gave Sikkim internal sovereignty, but what would be internal sovereignty in absence of external sovereignty. Subjects of Sikkim were to be represented as Indian in abroad (Article IV); this clause violated the very identity of Sikkim as an international entity. If Maxwell contends that this treaty was designed to degrade Sikkim into India in a true imperialistic manner, then he may not be wrong. And Mr. Rumbold's view that the action of India was a considerable extension of the 'theory of intervention' which they had developed already in relation to other acceding States, it seems to be taken out from the right inference. If one contends that this action of India was a first step towards making Sikkim full-fledged state of India, then he/she may not be wrong.

But it is said, most of these criticisms were exaggerated and emanated after the two decades of development by Indian help, guidance and assistance to the Kingdom of Sikkim which brought Sikkim to the forefront of the Himalayan belt of states (Grover 1974: 97), unlike Bhutan under the terms of the 1949 friendship treaty between India and Bhutan, having decided through mutual consent, to update the 1949 treaty relating to the promotion of, and fostering the relations of friendship and neighbourliness between India and Bhutan in 2007 (India - Bhutan Friendship Treaty 2007). But its essential status is much higher than that of a protectorate. India has refrained from interfering in its internal affairs and all this is of course subject to India's responsibility for the maintenance of law and order in the State. The treaty of 1949 and upgradation of this treaty in 2007, safeguarded the national interests of both the countries. It is a harsh reality that Sikkim could not maintain its separate identity and had to succumb under Indian Union, for the fact that India could not allow Sikkim to go under the Chinese influence without jeopardising the security of West Bengal, Assam and Arunachal Pradesh (Grover 1974: 97-98).

Conclusion

As Grover (1974) points out, the Nehru's inheritance of the British psychology of buffer zones influenced India to accord Sikkim a – special status. Gradually Sikkim became an Indian protectorate. The rising up of China as Communist State in the neighbourhood and subsequent takeover of Tibet, prompted India to negotiate its position vis-à-vis Sikkim. It led to the Treaty of 1950 which allowed India to look after the defence, communications, and foreign relations of the State.

After the independence of India, Great Britain was not in a position to accord Sikkim a new status since all the treaties between British, Princely States and Eastern Himalayan states were cancelled, and there was no question of continuance of Anglo-Sikkimese relations. Sikkim's strategic position would have cost India a great setback if there was a continuance of British-Sikkim relations. That is the reason why Great Britain had to leave everything in the hands of India, to decide what would be the position of Sikkim vis-à-vis independent India. Under the changed situation, Sikkim was granted 'special position' vis-à-vis Indian Princely States because of its strategic location.

As pointed out by Risley in 1894, that "the peculiar position of Sikhim (Sikkim) renders it impossible for us to ignore it as we ignore Bhutan, or to treat it on terms of comparative equality as we treat Nepal. Sikkim cannot stand by itself, and if we withdraw our support, it must ultimately fall either to Tibet/China or to Nepal". As history proved, Sikkim, the small Himalayan Kingdom surrounded by foreign countries by four sides, ultimately had to succumb under the Indian Union becoming the twenty second state on 16th May 1975.

CHAPTER V

Conclusion

This book after discussing the patterns, dynamics and dimensions of the relation with Great Britain in the colonial times has come up with the conclusion that, Sikkim had a unique position under British Imperial Raj in India. Sikkim was neither a colony, nor outside the zone of influence of British. Sikkim, along with other Eastern Himalayan States, was at the periphery of the British colonial interest and it was treated as a peripheral state, heavily dependent to Great Britain in terms of political and economic survival. To address this unique position, this work connotes Sikkim with the term – colonial periphery – which means a state neither under colonialism nor outside the zone of influence of colonialism and predominantly acts according to the aspirations of colonial master.

In the chapters, we have seen the interactions between Sikkim and Great Britain for almost 130 years, and also in what circumstances Sikkim came into contact with Great Britain. We have also seen what lasting impacts British on Sikkim after coming into contact with Sikkim. When Britain came into contact with Sikkim, *The Great Game* was going on in Central Asia. *The Great Game* was played between British Empire and Russian Empire for the supremacy of Central Asia. Great Britain's strategy in the

Great Game was mainly to keep the Russian (earlier the Tsar and later the Communist) Empire away from India and therefore, Sikkim was important in the British plans in the Himalayas. Sikkim was on Lenin's classic route of communist conquest as for Lenin 'the road to Paris lies through Peking and Calcutta'. Sikkim was regarded as a mountain highway to Calcutta. The position of Sikkim was as such, if Russia had gained prominence over Sikkim, then it would have had upper hand in the Great Game against Britain. But in the case of Sikkim, during colonial times, no other power gained prominence over Sikkim except Britain. Britain even stopped the penetration of Russia into Tibet. Resultantly, Russians never came closer to Sikkim and never had a chance to penetrate into India through the mountain highways in Sikkim.

The contact between Sikkim and Britain can be traced back to 1814 in the Anglo-Gorkha war, and after the signing of Treaty of Titaliya in 1817, Sikkim entered into an official pact with Great Britain. The establishment of a rudimentary administration in Sikkim can be traced back to 1890s, in the time of Claude White, who was the first Political Officer of Sikkim. Under his initiative, a Council was formed to look after the affairs of Sikkim. The Council was composed of Rajah, Phodang Lama and Dorje Lopen to represent the Lamas, Khangsa Dewan, Purboo Dewan, Gangtok Kazi and Tashiding Kazi to represent the lay interests, Shew Dingpon as the writer and White himself as the Chairman. The Council's functions were to collect revenues, listen to appeals of laymen and women and to manage the day-to-day affairs of the state. Since, appointing the Political Officer in Sikkim, the British observed that to promote their interests in Sikkim they have to wipe out the pro-Tibetan institutions from Sikkim.

Lepchas were the first, who settled in Sikkim followed by Bhutias and Nepalese. It is argued that, the Bhutias destroyed the Lepcha literature containing their traditions and creed and translated into Lepcha tradition their own mythological works. Bhutias invented a new literature for Lepchas, in which they replaced Lepcha literature by their own literature, and asked them to follow the new rituals. Bhutias did so to establish their own institutions wiping out the Lepcha tradition. And much later, British also did the same by bringing up the leading families of Bhutia aristocracy into English education to eradicate the pro-Tibetan institutions and to build their own institution based on English education. The Kazis and Lamas were the indigenous aristocrats of Sikkim and by bringing up their sons and daughters in English education, British wanted to create a section of pro-British aristocrats.

Sikkim as a 'colonial periphery' did not have the power to bargain with Britain. After the cutting off of Maharajah's allowance for an interim period due to disturbed political situation, Sikkim literally became paralysed and had to accede to the demands of the British Government. Sikkim accepted whatever privileges offered by Britain. British India made Sikkim how it wanted to be – an outpost – guarding British interests in India, which they considered as Jewel in their Crown. British Government at times used coercive means and even direct force to bring Sikkim under their control. The Maharajah along with royal family was sent to exile when Maharajah did not abide by the clauses laid down in the 1861 treaty. The whole state was ruled by the

Political Officer with the help of Council for nearly six years. Grover (1974) says after the independence of India, India not only inherited specific treaties governing its relationship with Tibet and Sikkim, but it inherited a fundamental geographical situation which neither the independence of India nor the communist revolution in China changed.

Literature says that 'the process of colonising Sikkim was over in 1904 in every respect with the signing of Lhasa Convention'. But, technically Sikkim was never a colony of British Empire. Rather, British kept Sikkim as a "colonial periphery". British never colonised Sikkim, for the fact that British wanted to create a belt of buffer states to protect their interests from the Tsarist Russia and China. The Eastern Himalayan states were shaped in a manner that they were under the zone of influence of Great Britain but they were not the colonies of Britain.

The reason for keeping Sikkim as a colonial periphery is also very clear. Had Sikkim been colonised by the British, then the British would have come into a direct confrontation with Tibet/China. Tibet was not happy with the meddling of British in Sikkim affairs since it considered Sikkim a part of it. And, in terms of size, British were gaining nothing by colonising Sikkim. If British had come into direct contact with Tibet/China then they would had to maintain a huge army to prevent Sikkim from Tibet/China and even Russia, which they wanted to avoid. British Government influenced by these arguments, thought it necessary to continue its connection with Sikkim as a colonial periphery.

Surjit Mansingh (1984) says 'Sikkim was listed as an Indian Princely State in the India Act of 1935'. Actually, there is no such list in the Act of 1935 which lists Sikkim as a princely state. The Act of 1935 did not make Sikkim a princely state or part of India. In the Act of 1935, the British divided states into three categories namely: a) British India, b) India and c) Indian State. "British India" meant provinces under Governors, "India" contains those states with Rulers who were under Governor General directly and lastly, "Indian State" was 'any territory, whether described as a State, an Estate, a Jagir or otherwise, belonging to or under the suzerainty of a Ruler who is under the suzerainty of King of Britain and not being part of British India'.

The administrative arrangement was such that the British India and India were under the authority of Governor General directly. States under Indian State and not part of either of the first two categories were subjected to the authority of Secretary of State. Sikkim was under the authority of Secretary of State. There was a provision that states under Indian State can become part of India or come under Indian federation when a Ruler by the virtue of Instrument of Accession accedes his/her state to the Indian federation. Maharajah of Sikkim had never done this and the implication of this was Sikkim remained in the Indian State therefore subjected to the authority of Secretary of State, not subjected to the authority of Governor General, who dealt with the states under British Empire.

States which had come under the federation of India and under British India had to send two representatives to the Council of State and the Federal Assembly. It is also to be noted that Sikkim never sent any representative to either Council or Assembly. It was decided that, in the interests of India and Sikkim, the existing posts concerned with Sikkim's political relations would continue to be maintained under the control of the External Affairs Department in Delhi. Sikkim was under the authority of Political Officer, and Political Officer was answerable to the Ministry of External Affairs, Government of India. After the independence of India, states under British India and India in the Act of 1935 were merged into the Indian Union but Sikkim was not merged into the Indian Union. Government of India recognised the sovereignty of Sikkim and in 1950 it entered into an agreement with Sikkim making Sikkim a 'protectorate state' of Indian Union. Throughout this period, Sikkim remained a subject under Ministry of External Affairs, Government of India, and Political Office in Sikkim was continued till its merger with India to 1975.

It was clear that, after the termination of British paramountcy in India, all the treaties signed between British Government, Princely States and Eastern Himalayan states became null and void. The Memorandum of the Cabinet Mission underlines this as, 'with the attainment of independence by British India, the relationship which existed between the Rulers of the states, both inside and outside the British Crown will no longer be possible. Paramountcy can neither be retained nor transferred to the new Government'. By the end of Second World War the British imperial interest in the region became a question of less relevance. Independent India took over the relations from British Government and Indian interests became the deciding factor in the future relations of these states.

When Constituent Assembly was created in 1946, Nehru knew that the committee set up for the purpose of discussing terms with the Rulers of Princely States, would have no authority to discuss the terms with Sikkim and

Bhutan. Therefore, additional power was ascribed to the committee: it was to negotiate with territories which are not Indian States; Bhutan and Sikkim.

With the withdrawal of British from South Asia, India was at the core of the relations with the Princely States and Eastern Himalayan States. India became an undisputed power in the region. Therefore, the transfer of the authority from Colonial Crown to India became inevitable because British Government did not transfer the paramountcy to India. General Assembly treated India as a successor to pre-1947 India and admitted Pakistan as a new member in the United Nations. In International Law, the laws of the predecessor state remains in force until the new sovereign takes step to change it, survival of the old laws depends on the consent of the new sovereign.

State succession arises when there is absolute replacement of one state by another (Brownlie 2008: 649-65). British completely pulled it out of the region and did not retain any relation that it had with the states under its paramountcy or the states outside the paramountcy. Since Sikkim decided to keep the Office of Political Officer and also entered into the same kind of relation with India which she had with Britain it can be concluded that India replaced Britain. India inherited the relation which the British had with Sikkim and Sikkim recognised the protectorate right of India over it which made clarity over the future relation of Sikkim and India on the one hand and Sikkim and Britain on the other after the withdrawal of Britain from South-Asia.

To conclude, this study has tried to look upon the British influence in the region by making use of existing literature, sources in local languages and archival materials.

But still much work remains to be done on the said theme as pointed out by scholars like Alex McKay. McKay talks about the East India Company Archives in Rangpur (Bangladesh), which could cover the period between 1750-1850, which is not been looked by any academicians till now. This work tried to provide answers to the questions on British influence in shaping the politics of the region and its impact on the state of Sikkim. Over all, this study makes the conclusion that the regional, political, economic, and strategic interests of British colonialism played a key role in determining the political developments and present political situation in Sikkim.

REFERENCES

Primary Sources

Section One: The Records and Documents from Sikkim State Archives

List of Old Tibetan papers about the War between British and Tibetan Governments; received from the Office of the Political Officer in Sikkim. 18/09/1916

Appointment regarding Civil and Military Office under the Crown, 21/06/1916.

Demarcation of Agency and Residency Compound, 16/8(i)/1916.

Transfer of Control of Excise, Income Tax, Police, Jail, Judicial and Revenue Stamp Department to H. H., 27/03/1916.

Viceroy's letter regarding War with Afghanistan, 9/05/1919.

Maharajah's acknowledgement of receiving of Viceroy's letter regarding War with Afghanistan, 18/05/1919.

Peace Celebration, 12/4(XII)/1919.

In view of the signing of the Peace Treaty between the Allies and Germany, Maharajah's order regarding Special Peace Prayers in all the Monasteries in Sikkim, 3/07/1919.

Inauguration Ceremony of Chamber of Princes at Delhi, 22/11(XXII)/1920.

Reply to the Viceroy's Letter of 22/11/1920. Regarding the Inauguration Ceremony of

Chamber of Princes at Delhi, 9/10/1920.

H. H.'s order on Resignation of Chief Court Members from the Council, 10/5(V)/1923

H. H.'s order on Retention of his Council, 29/09/1922.

In a reply from the Political Officer's Office regarding H. H.'s order on Retention of his Council of 29/09/1922, 28/03/1923.

Section Two: Treaties, Deeds, Conventions, and Agreements

Treaty of Sugauli, 2nd December 1815 between East India Company and the country of Nepal

Treaty between the Raja of Sikkim and Government of India, 10 February 1817

The Deed of the Grant Making over Darjeeling to the East India Company, 1835

Treaty of Tumlong 1861

Convention of 4 March 17th 1890 between Great Britain and China relating to Sikkim and Tibet (Ratification exchanged at London, August 27th, 1890)

Convention between Great Britain and Tibet, Signed at Lhasa on the 7th September, 1904.

Convention between Great Britain and China, Dated 27th April, 1906. (Received in London, 18th June, 1906.)

Convention between Great Britain and Russia, 1907.

Government of India, Act of 1935

Indo-Sikkim Treaty of 1950

Section Three: Gazetteers

Hamilton, W. (1828): *The East Indian Gazetteer,* London, Parbury, Allen and Co.

Hunter, W. W. (1887): *The Imperial Gazetteer of India: Volume XII, Ratlam to Sirmur,* London, Trubner and co.

Risley, H. H. (1894/1989): *The Gazetteer of Sikhim,* Calcutta, The Bengal Secretariat Press.

Section Four: Interviews

Interview with Honourable Member of Parliament (MP) Shri P. D. Rai on December 29, 2013.

Interviews with Shri C. D. Rai on December 29, 2013 and February 15, 2014.

Secondary Sources

Abilov, S. *The "New Great Game" Over the Caspian Region: Russia, the USA, and China in the Same Melting Pot.* Retrieved on 21/11/2013, URL: jhss-khazar.org/.../New-Great-Game.pdf

Aloysius, G. (1997/1998/2008): *Nationalism without a Nation in India,* New Delhi, Oxford University Press.

Arthur Connolly. Retrieved on 27/12/2013, URL: http://en.wikipedia.org/wiki/The-Great-Game)

Assistant Secretary at India Office. Retrieved on 27/02/2014, URL: www.indpendent.co.uk/news/people/obituary-sir-algernon-rumbold-1465721.html

Balikci-Denjongpa, A. and McKay, A. (Eds.) (2011): *Buddhist Himalaya: Studies in Religion, History and Culture,* Gangtok, Namgyal Institue of Tibetology.

Bhanja, K. (1993): *History of Darjeeling and the Sikkim Himalaya,* New Delhi, Gyan Publishing House.

Bondarevsky, G. L. (2002): *The Great Game: A Russian Perspective*, East Sussex, Christie Books.

Brownlie, I. (2008). *Principles of Public International Law,* New York, Oxford University Press.

Central Asia and the Great Games: Different Times, the Same Game?. Retrieved on 15/01/2014, URL: rc41.ipsa.org/public/Madrid.../duarte.pdf

Chopra, P. (1979): *Sikkim*, New Delhi, S.Chand.

Das, B. S. (1983): *The Sikkim Saga,* Ghaziabad, Vikas Publishing House Pvt. Ltd.

Datta-Ray, S. K. (1984/2004): *Smash and Grab: Annexation of Sikkim,* Delhi, Vikas Publishing House Pvt. Ltd.

Edgar, J. W. (1969): *Report on a visit to Sikhim and the Thibetan Frontier,* New Delhi, Manjusri Publishing House.

English, R. (1985): "Himalayan State Formation and the Impact of British Rule in the Nineteenth Century", *Mountain Research and Development, Vol. 5, No. 1*, 61-78.

Furber, H. (1951). "The Unification of India, 1947-1951", *Pacific Affairs, Vol. 24, No. 4 (Dec., 1951).*

Grover, B. (1974): *Sikkim and India: Storm and Consolidation,* New Delhi, Jain Brothers.

HELP FOR RESEARCHERS. Retrieved on 14/01/2014, URL: www.bl.uk/reshelp/findhelpregion/asia/india/politsecrec/index.html

HELP FOR RESEARCHERS. Retrieved on 14/01/2014, URL: www.bl.uk/reshelp/findHelpregion/asia/india/indiaofficerecords/indiaofficehub.html

Hopkirk, P. (1990): *The Great Game; On Secret Service in high Asia.* Retrieved on 05/01/2014, URL: <u>pamirs.org/ Extract%20Odyssey%20Great%20Game.pdf</u>

Jha, P. K. (1985): *History of Sikkim (1817-1904): Analysis of British Policy and Activities,* Calcutta, O P S Publishers Private Ltd.

Jian, C. (2006): "The Tibetan Rebellion of 1959 and China's: Changing Relations with India and the Soviet Union", *Journal of Cold War Studies, Vol. 8, No. 3, Summer 2006,* 54-101.

Kotturan, G. (1983): *The Himalayan Gateway: History and Culture of Sikkim,* New Delhi, Sterling Publishers.

Lamb, A. (1964): *The China-Indian Border: The Origin of the Disputed boundaries,* London, Oxford University Press.

Lebedeva, N. (1965). "British colonial policy in Sikkim", *Central Asian Rev.13,* 258–266.

Lepcha, P. N. (2011/2013). "Lepchas - A Cultural Perspective", S. P. Wangdi (Eds.), *Sikkim's Raj Bhavan* (pp. 65-74), Gangtok, Department of Information and Public Relations.

Levi, W. (1959). "Bhutan and Sikkim: Two Buffer States", *The World Today, Vol. 15, No. 12 (Dec., 1959), pp. 492-500.*

Mansingh, S. (1984). *India's Search for Power: Indira Gandhi's Foreign Policy 1966-1982,* New Delhi, Sage Publications India Pvt. Ltd.

McKay, A. (1997). *Tibet and the British Raj,* Dharamsala, Indraprastha Press.

McKay, A. (1997): "Tibet 1924: A Very British Coup Attempt?", *Journal of the Royal Asiatic Society, Third Series, Vol. 7, No. 3*, 411-24.

Meyer, K. (2005): *In the Shadows of the Himalayas: Tibet, Bhutan, Nepal and Sikkim,* Ahmedabed, Mapin Publishing Pvt. Ltd.

Morgan, G. (1973). "Myth and Reality in the Great Game", *Asian Affairs Volume 4, Issue 1, 1973.*

Mullard, S. and Wongchuk, H. (2010): *Royal Records: A Catalogue of the Sikkimese Palace Archive,* Andiast, International Institute for Tibetan and Buddhist Studies.

Mullard, S. (2011): *Opening the Hidden Land: State Formation and the Construction of Sikkimese History,* Boston, Brill.

Namgyal Dynasty. Retrieved on 28/03/2014, 2014, URL: www. tibetology.net/researchprojects/visualsikkim/namgyaldynasty2. html

Namgyal, T. and Dolma, Y. (1908): *History of Sikkim,* Gangtok, Unpublished Typescrript.

Phadnis, U. (1980): "Ethnic Dimensions of Sikkimese Politics: The 1979 Elections", *Asian Survey, Vol. 20, No. 12 (Dec., 1980), pp. 1236-1252*

Pradhan, K. C. (2011/2013): "Reflections on the Political Officers and Governors", S. P. Wangdi (Eds.), *Sikkim's Raj Bhavan* (pp. 219-229), Gangtok, Department of Information and Public Relations.

Rai, C. D. (2011/2013) "India's Independence and its Impact on Sikkim", S. P. Wangdi (Eds.), *Sikkim's Raj Bhavan* (pp. 101-106), Gangtok, Department of Information and Public Relations.

Rao, P. R. (1972): *India and Sikkim (1814-1970),* New Delhi, Sterling Publishers (P) Ltd.

Rock, J. F. (1953). "Excerpts from a History of Sikkim", *Anthropos Institute*, 925-948.

Rustomji, N. (1987): *Sikkim - A Himalayan Tragedy,* New Delhi, Allied Publishers.

Sharma, S. K. (Eds.) (1998): *Documents on Sikkim and Bhutan,* New Delhi, Anmol Publications Pvt. Ltd.

Sharma, S. K. (Eds.) (1998): *History Geography and Travels of Sikkim and Bhutan,* New Delhi, Anmol Publications Pvt. Ltd.

Sharma, T. (1996): *Sikkim: Hija Dekhi Aja Samma,* Gangtok, Ankur Publication.

Singh, A. K. (1988): *Himalayan Triangle: A Historical Survey of British india's Relations with Tibet, Sikkim and Bhutan (1765-1950),* London, The British Library.

Sinha, A. C. (2008): *Sikkim: Feudal and Democratic,* New Delhi, Indus Publishing House.

Smith D. L. *Central Asia: A New Great Game?* Retrieved on 22/11/2013, URL: http://www.jstor.org/stable/30172401

Temple, R. (1977): *Travels in Nepal and Sikkim,* Kathmandu, Ratna Pustak Bhandar.

Vajracharya, D. and Shresta, T. B: "Political Asylum of Kazi Yukla Thup of Sikkim in Nepal", Unpublished Typescript.

Wangdi, S. (Eds.) (2011/2013): *Sikkim's Raj Bhawan,* Gangtok, Department of Information and Public Relations.

White, J. C. (1909/1999/2008): *Sikhim and Bhutan: Twenty-One Years on the North-East Frontier (1887-1908),* Delhi, Low Price Publications.

Younghusband, S. F. (1910/1994/2002): *India and Tibet,* Delhi, Low Price Publication.

ANNEXURE I

TREATY OF SUGAULI, 2nd DECEMBER 1815 BETWEEN EAST INDIA COMPANY AND THE COUNTRY OF NEPAL

TREATY of PEACE between the HONOURABLE EAST INDIA COMPANY AND MAHARAJAH BIRKRAM SAH, Rajah of Nipal, settled between LIEUTENANT –COLONEL BRADSHAW on the part of the HONOURABLE COMPANY, in virtue of the full powers vested in him by HIS EXCELLENCY the RIGHT HONOURABLE FRANCIS, EARL of MOIRA, KNIGHT of the MOST NOBLE ORDER of the GARTER, one of HIS MAJESTY's MOST HONOURABLE PRIVY COUNCIL, appointed by the Court of Directors of the said Honourable Company to direct and control all the affairs in the East Indies, and by SREE GOOROO GUJRAJ MISSER and CHUNDER SEEKUR OPEDEEA on the part of MAHA RAJAH GIRMAUN JODE BIKRAM SAH BAHAUDER, SHUMSHEER JUNG, in virtue of the powers to that effect vested in them by the said Rajah of Nipal, 2nd December 1815.

Whereas war has arisen between the Honourable East India Company and the Rajah of Nipal, and whereas the parties are mutually disposed to restore the relations of peace and amity which, previously to the occurrence of the late differences, had long subsisted between the two States, the following terms of peace have been agreed upon:

ARTICLE I

There shall be perpetual peace and friendship between the Honourable East India Company and the Rajah of Nipal.

ARTICLE II

The Rajah of Nipal renounces all claim to the lands which were the subject of discussion between the two States before the war, and acknowledges the right of the Honourable Company to the sovereignty of those lands.

ARTICLE III

The Rajah of Nipal hereby cedes to the Honourable the East India Company in perpetuity all the under-mentioned territories, viz-

First: – The whole of the low lands between the Rivers Kali and Rapti.

Secondly: – The whole of the low lands (with the exception of Bootwul Khass) lying between the Rapti and the Gunduck.

Third: The whole of the low lands between the Gunduck and Coosah, in which the authority of the British Government has been introduced, or is in actual course of introduction.

Fourth: All the low lands between the Rivers Mitchee and the Teestah.

Fifth: All the territories within the hills eastward of the River Mitchee including the fort and lands of Nagree and the Pass of Nagarcote leading from Morung into the hills, together with the territory lying between that pass and nagerr. The aforesaid territory shall be evacuated by the Gurkha troops within forty days form this date.

ARTICLE IV

With a view to indemnify the Chiefs and Barahdars of the State of Nipal, whose interests will suffer by the alienation of the lands ceded by the foregoing Article, the British Government agrees to settle pensions to the aggregate amount of two lakhs of rupees per annum on such Chiefs as may be selected by the Rajah of Nipal, and in the proportions which the Rajah may fix. As soon as the selection is made, Sunnuds shall be granted under the seal and signature of the Governor General for the pensions respectively.

ARTICLE V

The Rajah of Nipal renounces for himself, his heirs, and successors, all claim to or connextion with the countries lying to the west of the River Kali and engages never to have any concern with those countries or the inhabitants there of.

ARTICLE VI

The Rajah of Nipal engages never to molest to disturb the Rajah of Sikkim in the possession of his territories; but agrees, if any difference shall arise between the State of Nipal and the Rajah of Sikkim, or the subjects of either, that such differences shall be referred to the arbitration of the British Government by which award the Rajah of Nipal engages to abide.

ARTICLE VII

The Rajah of Nipal hereby engages never to take of retain in his service any British subject, nor the subject of any European or American State, without the consent of the British Government.

ARTICLE VIII

In order to secure and improve the relations of amity and peace hereby established between the two States, it is agreed that accredited Ministers from each shall reside at the Court of the other.

ARTICLE IX

This treaty, consisting of nine Articles, shall be ratified by the Rajah of Nipal within fifteen days from this date, and the ratification shall be delivered to Lieutenant-Colonel Bradshaw, who engages to obtain and deliver the ratification of the Governor-General within twenty days, or sooner, if practicable.

Done at Segowlee, on the 2nd day of December 1815.

PARIS BRADSHAW, Lt. Col., P.A.

Received this treaty from Chunder Seekur Opedeea, Agent on the part of the Rajah Nipal, in the valley of Muckwaunpoor, at half-past two o'clock p.m. on the 4th of March 1816, and delivered to him the Counterpart Treaty on behalf of the British Government.

D.D. OCHTERLONY,
Agent, Governor-General.

ANNEXURE II

Treaty between the Raja of Sikkim and Government of India, 10 February 1817

TREATY, COVENANT, or AGREEMENT entered into by CAPTAIN BARRE LATTER, AGENT on the part of HIS EXCELLENCY the RIGHT HONORABLE the EARL of MOIRA, K.G., GOVERNOR-GENERAL, &c., &c., &c., &c., and by NAZIR CHAINA TENJIN and MACHA TEINBAH and LAMA DUCHIM LONGDOO, Deputies on the part of the RAJAH Of SIKKIMPUTTEE, being severally authorized and duly appointed for the above purposes, 1817.

ARTICLE 1.

The Honorable East India Company cedes, transfers, and makes over in full sovereignty to the Sikkimputtee Rajah, his heirs or successors, all the hilly or mountainous country situated to the eastward of the Mechi River and to the westward of the Teesta River, formerly possessed and occupied by the Rajah of Nepaul, but ceded to the Honorable East India Company by the Treaty of peace signed at Segoulee.

ARTICLE 2.

The Sikkimputtee Rajah engages for himself and successors to abstain from any acts of aggression or hostility against the Goorkhas or any other State.

ARTICLE 3.

That he will refer to the arbitration of the British Government any disputes or questions that may arise between his subjects and those of Nepaul, or any other neighbouring State, and to abide by the decision of the British Government.

ARTICLE 4.

He engages for himself and successors to join the British Troops with the whole of his Military Force when employed within the Hills, and in general to afford the British Troops every aid and facility in his power.

ARTICLE 5.

That he will not permit any British subject, nor the subject of any European and American State, to reside within his dominions, without the permission of the English Government.

ARTICLE 6.

'That he will immediatley seize and deliver up any dacoits or notorious offenders that may take refuge within his territories.

ARTICLE 7.

That he will not afford protection to any defaulters of revenue or other delinquents when demanded by the British Government through their accredited Agents.

ARTICLE 8.

That he will afford protection to merchants and traders from the Company's Provinces, and he engages that no duties shall be levied on the transit of merchandize beyond the established custom at the several golahs or marts.

ARTICLE 9.

The Honorable East India Company guarantees to the Sikkimputtee Rajah and his successors the full and peaceable possession of the tract of hill country specified in the first Article of the present Agreement.

ARTICLE 10.

This Treaty shall be ratified and exchanged by the Sikkimputtee Rajah within one month from the present date, and the counterpart, when confirmed by His Excellency the Right Honorable the Governor-General, shall be transmitted to the Rajah.

Done at Titalya, this 10th day of February 1817, answering to the 9th of Phagoon 1873 Sumbut, and to the 30th of Maugh 1223 Bengallie.

BARRE LATTER.
NAZIR CHAINA TINJIN.
MACHA TIMBAH.
LAMA DUCHIM LONGADOC.

MOIRA.
N. B. EDMONSTONE.
ARCHD. SETON.
GEO. DOWDESWELL.

Ratified by the Governor-General in Council, at Fort William, this fifteenth day of March, one thousand eight hundred and seventeen.

J. ADAM,
Acting Chief Secy. to Govt.

ANNEXURE III

Treaty of Tumlong 1861

Treaty, Covenant or Agreement entered into by the Hon'ble Ashley Edenm, envoy and special Commissioner on the part of the British Government, in virtue of full powers vested in him by the Right Hon'ble Charles, Earl Canning, Governor-General in Council, and by His Highness Sekeong Kuzoo, Maharajah of Sikkim on his own part, 1861.

Whereas the continued depredation and misconduct of the officers and subjects of the Maharajan of Sikkim, and the neglect of the Maharajah to afford satisfaction for the misdeeds of his people have resulted in an interruption for many years past of the harmony which previously existed between the British Government and the Government of Sikkim, and have led ultimately to the invasion and conquest of Sikkim by a British force, and whereas the Maharajah of Sikkim has now expressed his sincere regret for the misconduct off his servants and subjects, his determination to do all in his power to obviate future misunderstanding and his desire to be again admitted into friendship and alliance with the British Government, it is hereby agreed as follows.

Article I

All previous Treaties made between the British Government and the Sikkim Government are hereby formally cancelled.

Article II

The whole of the Sikkim territory now in the occupation of British forces is restored to the Maharajah of Sikkim, and there shall henceforth be peace and amity between the two states.

Article III

The Maharajah of Sikkim undertakes, so far as is within his power, to restore within one month from the date of signing this Treaty, all public property which was abandoned by the detachment of British troops at Rinchenpong.

Article IV

In indemnification of the expenses incurred in 1860 by the British Government in occupying portion of the territory of Sikkim as a means of enforcing just claim's which had been evaded by the Government of Sikkim, and as compensation to the British subjects who were pillaged and kidnapped by subjects of Sikkim, tile Sikkim Government agrees to pay to the British authorities at Darjeeling the sum of 7000 (seven thousand) rupees in the following instalments, that is to say:

May 1st, 1861 Rs.l000.

Nov 1st, 1861 Rs.3000.

May 1st, 1862 Rs.3000.

As security for the due payment of this amount, it is further agreed that in the event of any of these instalments not being duly paid on the date appointed the Government of Sikkim shall make over to the British government that portion of its territory bounded on the south by the river Rummam, on the east by the great Runjeet river, on the north by a line from the Great Runjeet to the Singaleelah Range, including the monasteries of Tassiding, Pemonchi, and changacheling, and on the west by the Singaleelah Mountain Range, and the British Government shall retain possession of this territory and collect the revenue thereof, until the full amount, with all expenses of occupation and collection, and interest at 6 per cent annum, are realized.

Article V

The Government of Sikkim engages that its subjects shall never again commit depredations on British territory, or kidnap or otherwise molest British subjects. In the event of any such depredation or kidnapping taking place, the Government of Sikkim undertakes to deliver up all persons engaged in such malpractice, as well a the Sirdars or other chiefs conniving at or benefiting thereby.

Article VI

The Government of Sikkim will at all times seize and deliver up any criminals, Defeaters, or other delinquents who may have taken refuge within Its territory, on demand being duly made in writing by the British government through their accredited agents. Should any delay occur in complying with such demand, the police of the British Government may follow the person whose surrender has been demanded into any part of the Sikkim territory and shall, on showing a warrant, duly signed by the British agent, receive every assistance and protection in the prosecution of their object from the Sikkim officers.

Article VII

In as rnuch as the late rnisunderstandmgs between the two Governrnents have been mainly fomented by the acts of the ex-Dewan Namguay, the Governrnent of Sikkim engages that neither the said Namguay, nor any of his blood relations, shall ever again be allowed to set foot in Sikkim, or to take part in the councils of, or hold any office under, the Maharajah or any of the Maharajah's family at Choombi.

Article VIII

The Government of Sikkim from this date abolishes all restrictions on travelers and monopolies in trade between the British territories and Sikkim. There shall henceforth be a free reciprocal intercourse, and full liberty of commerce between the subjects of both countries; it shall be lawful for British subjects to go into any part of Sikkim for the purpose of navel or trade, and the subjects of all countries shall be permitted to reside in and pass through Sikkim, and to expose their goods for sale at any place and in any manner that may best suit their purpose, Without any interference whatever, except as is hereinafter provided.

Article IX

The Governrnent of Sikkim engages to afford protection to all travelers, merchants or traders of all countries, whether residing in, trading in, or passing through Sikkim. If any merchant, traveler or trader, being a European British subject, shall commit any offence contrary to the laws of Sikkim, such person shall be punished by the representative of the British Governrnent resident at Darjeeling, and the Sikkim Government will at once deliver such offender over to the British authorities for this purpose, and will on no account, detain such offender in Sikkim on any pretext or pretence whatever. All other British subjects residing in the country to be liable to the laws of Sikkim; but such persons shall, on no account, be punished with loss of limb, or maiming or torture and every case of punishment of a British subject shall be at once reported to Darjeeling.

Article X

No duties or fees of any sort shall be demanded by the Sikkim Governrnent of any person or persons on account of goods exported into the British territories from Sikkim, or imported into Sikkim from the British territories.

Article XI

On all goods passing into or out of Tibet, Bhootan, or Nepal, the Government of Sikkim may levy a duty of customs according to such a scale as may, from time to time, be determined and published without reference to the destination of goods, provided, however, that such duty shall, on no account, exceed 5 percent on the value of goods at the time and place of the levy of duty. On the payment of the duty aforesaid a pass shall be given exempting such goods from liability to further payment on any account whatever.

Article XII

With the view to protect the Government of Sikkim from fraud on account of Undervaluation for assessment of duty, it is agreed that the customs officers shall have the option of taking over for the Government any goods at the value affixed on them by the owner.

Article XIII

In the event of the British Government desiring to open out a road through Sikkim, with the view of encouraging trade, the Sikkim Government will raise no objection thereto, and will afford every protection and aid to the party engaged in the work. If a road is constructed, the Government of Sikkim undertakes to keep it in repair, and to erect and maintain suitable travellers' rest-houses throughout its route.

Article XIV

If the British Government desires to make either a topographical or geological survey of Sikkim, the Sikkim Government will raise no objection to this being done, and will afford protection and assistance to the officers employed in this duty.

Article XV

In as much as many of the late misunderstandings have had foundation in the custom which exists in Sikkim of dealing in slaves, the Government of Sikkim binds itself, from this date, to punish severely any person trafficking in human beings, or seizing persons for the purpose of using them as slaves.

Article XVI

Henceforth the subjects of Sikkim may transport themselves without let or hi 1dranceto any country to which they may wish to remove. In the same way the Government of Sikkim has authority to permit the subjects of other countries, not being criminals or defaulters, to take refuge in Sikkim.

Article XVII

The Government of Sikkim engages to abstain from any act of aggression or hostility against any of the neighbouering states which are allies of the British Government. If any disputes or questions arise between the people of Sikkim and those of neighbouring states, such disputes or questions shall be referred to the arbitration of the British Government, and the Sikkim Government agrees to abide by the decision of the British Government.

Article XIX

The whole military force of Sikkim shall join and afford every aid and facility to British Troops when employed in the Hills.

Article XIX

The Government of Sikkim will not cede or lease any portion of its territory to any other state without the permission of the British Government.

Article XX

The Government of Sikkim engages that no armed force belonging to any other country shall pass through Sikkim without the sanction of the British Government.

Article XXI

Seven of the criminals, whose surrender was demanded by the British Government, having fled from Sikkim and taken refuge in Bhootan, the Government of Sikkim engages to do all in its power to obtain the delivery of those persons from the Bhootan Government, and in the event of any of these men again returning to Sikkim, the Sikkim Government binds itself to seize them and to make them over to the British Authorities at Darjeeling without delay.

Article XXII

With a view to the establishment of an efficient Government in Sikkim, and to the better maintenance of friendly relations with the British Government, the Maharajah of Sikkim agrees to remove the seat of his Government from Tibet to Sikkim, and reside there for nine months in the year. It is further agreed that a Vakeel shall be accredited by the Sikkim Government, who shall reside permanently at Darjeeling.

Article XXIII

This Treaty, consisting of twenty-three articles, being settled and concluded by the Honorable Ashley Eden, British Envoy, and His Highness Sekeong Kuzoo Sikkimputee, Maharajah, at Tumlong, this 28th day of March 1861, corresponding with 17 Dao Neeepoo 61, Mr. Eden has delivered to the Maharajaha copy of the same in English, with translation in Nagri and Bhootiah, under the seal arid signature of the said Honourable Asley Eden and His Highness the Sikkimputtee Maharajah, and the Sikkimputtee maharajah has in like manner delivered to said Hon'ble Asley Eden another copy also n English, with translation In Nagn and Bhoonsh, bearing the seal of His Highness and the said Hon'ble Asley Eden. The Envoy engages to procure the delivery to highness, Within Six weeks from this date, of a copy of this Treaty, duly ratifies by his Excellency the Viceroy and Governor General of India in Council and this treaty

Shall in the meantime be in full force.

Seal)
Sd)   **(Sd)**
Sekrong Kuzoo Sikkimputtee   **Asley Edan, Envoy**
Sd)

(Sd)
Canning   **(Seal)**

Ratified by his Excellency the Viceroy and Governor General of India in Council at Calcutta on the Sixteenth day of Apn1 1861.

(Sd)

C.U. Aitcheson
Under Secretary to the Government of India.

ANNEXURE IV

Convention of 4 March 17th 1890 between Great Britain and China relating to Sikkim and Tibet (Ratification exchanged at London, August 27th, 1890)

[English Text]

WHEREAS Her Majesty the Queen of the United Kingdom of Great Britain and Ireland, Empress of India, and His Majesty the Emperor of China, are sincerely desirous to maintain and perpetuate the relations of friendship and good understanding which now exist between their respective Empires and whereas recent occurrences have tended towards a disturbance of the said relations, and it is desirable to clearly define and permanently settle certain matters connected with the boundary between Sikkim and Tibet, Her Britannic Majesty and His Majesty the Emperor of China have resolved to conclude a Convention on this subject, and have, for this purpose, named Plenipotentiaries, that is to say: Her Majesty the Queen of Great Britain and Ireland, his Excellency the Most Honourable Henry Charles Keith Petty Fitzmaurice, G.M.S.L, G.C.M.G., G.M.LE., Marquees of Lansdowne, Viceroy and Governor-General of India; And His Majesty the Emperor of China, his Excellency Sheng Tai, Imperial Associate Resident in Tibet,

Military Deputy Lieutenant-Governor; Who, having met and communicated to each other their full powers, and finding these to be in proper form, have agreed upon the following Convention in eight Articles:-

I The boundary of Sikkim and Tibet shall be the crest of the mountain range separating the waters flowing into the Sikkim Teesta and its affluents from the waters flowing into the Tibetan Mochu and northwards into other rivers of Tibet. The line commences at Mount Gipmochi on the Bhutan frontier, and follows the above-mentioned water-parting to the point where it meets Nipal territory.

II. It is admitted that the British Government, whose Protectorate over the Sikkim State is hereby recognised, has direct and exclusive control over the internal administration and foreign relations of that State, and except through and with the permission of tile British Government neither the Ruler of the State nor any of its officers shall have official relations of any kind, formal or informal, with any other country.

Ill- The Government of Great Britain and Ireland and the Government of China engage reciprocally to respect the boundary as defined in Article I, and to prevent acts of aggressions from their respective sides of the frontier.

IV. The questions of providing increased facilities for trade across the Sikkim Tibet frontier will hereafter be discussed with a view to a mutually satisfactory arrangement by the High Contracting Powers.

V. The question of pasturage on the Sikkim side of the frontier is reserved for further examination and future adjustment.

VI. The High Contracting Powers reserve for discussion and arrangement the method in which official communications between the British authorities in India and the authorities in Tibet shall be conducted.

VII. Two joint Commissioners shall, within six months from the ratification of this Convention, be appointed, one by the British Government in India, the other by the Chinese Resident in Tibet. The said Commissioners shall meet and discuss the questions which, by the last three preceding Articles, have been reserved.

VIII. The present Convention shall be ratified, and the ratifications shall be exchanged in London as soon as possible after the date of the signature thereof. In witness whereof the respective negotiators have signed the same, and affixed thereunto the seals of their arms.

Done in quadruplicate at Calcutta, this 17th day of March, in the year of our Lord 1890, corresponding with the Chinese date, the 27th day of the second moon of the 16th year of Kuang Hsu.

LANSDOWNE
Signature of the Chinese Plenipotentiary.

ANNEXURE V

C. A. Bell, Esquire, C.I.E.,
Political Officer in Sikkim,

To

The Superintendent, Sikkim State,
Gangtok.

Dated Camp, viâ Gangtok, the 13th September 1916.

Sir,

I have the honour to state that from the records of my office it appears that in 1904 the strength of the Sikkim Military Police was increased by 20 temporary men on account of the Tibet Frontier Commission. The sanction of the Government of India (through the Bengal Government) has accorded to the supply on loan of 20 carbines and bayonets and necessary accessories with ammunition for the 20 temporary men, on the condition that these would be returned to the Fort William Arsenal, when the services of the temporary force had been dispensed with.

2. Would you kindly let me know whether the above-mentioned weapons, etc., have since been returned to the Fort William Arsenal or not; and, if not, how the matter stands?

I have the honour to be,
Sir,
Your most obedient servant,

C. Bell
Political Officer in Sikkim.

16/9/16.

ANNEXURE VI

Convention between Great Britain and Tibet
September 7th 1904

WHEREAS doubts and difficulties have arisen as to the meaning and validity of the Anglo-Chinese Convention of 1890, and the Trade Regulations of 1893, and as to the liabilities of the Tibetan Government under these Agreements; and whereas recent occurrences have tended towards a disturbance of the relations of friends hi p and good understanding which have existed between the British Government and the Government of Thibet; and whereas it is desirable to restore peace and amicable relations, and to resolve and determine the doubts and difficulties as aforesaid, the said Governments have resolved to conclude a Convention with these objects, and the following Articles have been agreed upon by Colonel F.E. Younghusband, C.I.E., in virtue of full of powers vested in him by His Britannic Majesty's Government, and on behalf of that said Government, and Losang Gyaltsen, The Ga-den Ti -Rimpoche, and the representatives of the council, of the three monasteries Se-ra, Dre-pung, and Ga-den, and of the ecclesiastical and lay officials of the National Assembly on behalf of the Government of Thibet:-

I. The Government of Thibet to engage to respect the Anglo-Chinese Convention of 1890, and to recognize the frontier between Sikkim and Thibet, as defined in Article I of the said Convention, and to erect boundary pillars accordingly.

II. The Thibetan Government undertakes to open forth with trade marts to which all British and Thibetan subjects shall have free right of access at Gyangtse and Gartok, as well as Yatung. The regulations applicable to the trade mart at Yatung, under the Anglo-Chinese Agreement of 1893, shall, subject to such amendments as may hereafter be agreed upon by common consent between the British and Thibetan Governments, apply to the marts above mentioned. In addition to establishing trade marts at the pl aces mentioned, the Thibetan Government undertakes to place no restrictions on the trade by existing routes, and to consider the question of establishing fresh trade marts under similar conditions if development of trade requires it.

III. The question of the amendment of the Regulations of 1893 is reserved for separate consideration, and the Thibetan Government undertakes to appoint fully authorized delegates to negotiate with representatives of the British Government as to the details of the amendments required.

IV. The Thibetan Government undertakes to levy no dues of any kind other than those provided for in the tariff to be mutually agreed upon.

V. The Thibetan Government undertakes to keep the roads to Gyangtse and Gartok from the frontier clear of all obstruction and in a state of repair suited to the needs of the trade, and to establish at Yatung, Gyangtse, and Gartok, and at each of the other trade marts that may hereafter be established, a Thibetan Agent who shall receive from the British Agent appointed to watch over British trade at the marts in question any letter which the latter may desire to send to the Thibetan or the Chinese authorities. The Thibetan Agent shall also be responsible for the due delivery of such communications and for the transmission of the replies.

VI. As an indemnity to the British Government for the expense incurred in the despatch of armed troops to Lhasa, to exact reparation for breaches of Treaty obligations, and for the insults offered to and attacks upon the British Commissioner and his following and escort, the Thibetan Government engages to pay a s um of 500,000-equivalent to 75 lakhs of rupees to the British Government. The indemnity shall be payable such place as the British Government may from time to time, after due notice, indicate, whether in Thibet or in the British districts of Darjeeling or Jalpaiguri, in seventy-five annual instalments of one lakh of rupees each on the 1s t January in each year, beginning from the 1s t January, 1906.

VII. As security for the payment of the above-mentioned indemnity, and for the fulfilment of the provisions relative to trade marts specified in Articles II, III, IV, and V, the British Government shall continue to occupy the Chumbi Valley until the indemnity has been paid, and until the trade marts have been effectively opened for three years, whichever date may be the later.

VIII. The Thibetan Government agrees to raze all forts and fortifications and remove all armaments which might impede the course of free communication between the British frontier and the towns of Gyangtse and Lhasa.

IX. The Government of Thibet engages that, without the previous consent of the British Government –

No portion of Thibetan territory shall be ceded, sold, leased, mortgaged or otherwise given for occupation, to any Foreign Power;

No such Power shall be permitted to intervene in Thibetan affairs;

No Representative or agents of any Foreign power shall be admitted to Thibet.

No concession for railways, roads, telegraphs, mining or other rights, shall be granted to any Foreign Power, or the subject of any Foreign Power. In the event of consent to such Concessions being granted, similar or equivalent Concessions shall be granted to the British Government; No Thibetan revenues, whether in kind or in cash, shall be pledged or assigned to any Foreign Power, or to the subject of any foreign power.

X. In witness whereof the negotiations have signed the same, and affixed thereunto the seals of their arms.

Done in quintuplicate at Lhasa, this 7th day of September, in the year of our Lord, 1904, corresponding with the Tibetan date, the 27th of the seventh month of the Wood Dragon year.

(Thibet Frontier Commission) F.E. YOUNG HUSBAND, Colonel, British Commissioner (Seal of Dalai Lama, affixed by the Ga-den Ti –Ri mpoche) (Seal of British Commissioner) (Seal of Dre-pung Monastery) (Seal of Sera Monastery) (Seal of Ga-den Monastery) (Seal of Ga-den Monastery)

In proceeding to the signature of the Convention, dated this day, the representatives of

Great Britain and Thibet declare that the English text shall be binding.

(Seal of Council) (Seal of Dre-pung Monastery) (Seal of Sera Monastery) (Seal of National Assembly)

In proceeding to the signature of the Convention, dated this day, the representatives of

Great Britain and Thibet declare that the English text shall be binding.

Thibet Frontier Commission) F.E. YOUNG HUSBAND, Colonel, British Commissioner (Seal of Dalai Lama affixed by the Ga-den Ti –Ri m poche) (Seal of Council) (Seal of Dre-pung Monastery) (Seal of Sera Monastery) (Seal of National Assembly)

AMPTHILL,
Viceroy and Governor-General of India

ANNEXURE VII

CONVENTION BETWEEN
GREAT BRITAIN AND CHINA
RESPECTING TIBET, APRIL 27, 1906

(Ratifications exchanged at London July 23 1906)
(British and Foreign State Papers, Vol. XCIX, pp. 171-173)

WHEREAS His Majesty of Great Britain and Ireland and of the British Dominions beyond the Seas, Emperor of India, and His Majesty the Emperor of China are sincerely desirous to maintain and perpetuate the relations of friendship and good understanding which now exists between their respective Empires;

And whereas the refusal of Tibet to recognise the validity of or to carry into full effect the provisions of the Anglo-Chinese Convention of March 17, 1890, and Regulations of December 5, 1893, placed the British Government under the necessity of taking steps to secure their rights and interests under the said Convention and Regulations;

And whereas a Convention of ten articles was signed at Lhasa on September 7, 1904, on behalf of Great Britain and Tibet, and was ratified by the Viceroy and Governor-General of India on behalf of Great Britain on November

11, 1904, a declaration on behalf of Great Britain modifying its terms under certain conditions being appended thereto;

His Britannic Majesty and His Majesty the Emperor of China have resolved to conclude a Convention on this subject and have for this purpose named Plenipotententiaries, that is to say:-

His Majesty the King of Great Britain and Ireland:

Sir Ernest Mason Satow, Knight Grand Cross of the Most Distinguished order of Saint Michael and Saint George, His said Majesty's Envoy Extra-ordinary and Minister Plenipotentiary to His Majesty the Emperor of China;

And His Majesty the Emperor of China:

His Excellency Tong Shoa-yi, His said Majesty's High Commissioner Plenipotentiary and a Vice-President of the Board of Foreign Affairs; who having communicated to each other their respective full powers and finding them to be in good and true form have agreed upon and concluded the following Convention in six articles:-

I. The Convention concluded on September 7, 1904, by Great Britain and Tibet, the texts of which in English and Chinese are attached to the present Convention as an annexe, is hereby confirmed, subject to the modification stated in the declaration appended thereto, and both of the High Contracting Parties engage to take at all times such steps as may be necessary to secure the due fulfilment of the terms specified therein.

II. The Government of Great Britain engages not to annex Tibetan territory or to interfere in the administration of Tibet. The Government of China also undertakes not to permit any other foreign state to interfere with the territory or internal administration of Tibet.

III. The Concessions which are mentioned in Article IX(d) of the Convention concluded on September 7th, 1904 by Great Britain and Tibet are denied to any state or to the subject of any state other than China, but it has been arranged with China that at the trade marts specified in Article II of the aforesaid Convention Great Britain shall be entitled to lay down telegraph lines connecting with India.

IV. The provisions of the Anglo-Chinese Convention of 1890 and Regulations of 1893 shall, subject to the terms of this present Convention and annexe thereto, remain in full force.

V. The English and Chinese texts of the present Convention have been carefully compared and found to correspond, but in the event of there being any difference of meaning between them the English text shall be authoritative.

VI. This Convention shall be ratified by the Sovereigns of both countries and ratifications shall be exchanged at London within three months after the date of signature by the Plenipotentiaries of both Powers.

In token whereof the repsrective Plenipotentiaries have signed and sealed this Convention, four copies in English and four in Chinese.

Done at Peking this twenty-seventh day of April, one thousand nine hundred and six, being the fourth day of the fourth month of the thirty-second year of the reign of KuangHsu.

ERNEST SATOW.
(Signature and Seal of the
Chinese Plenipotentiary)

ANNEXURE VIII

CONVENTION BETWEEN GREAT BRITAIN AND RUSSIA RELATING TO PERSIA, AFGHANISTAN AND TIBET, AUGUST 31, 1907

(As related to Tibet)

His Majesty the King of the United Kingdom of Great Britain and Ireland and of the British Dominions beyond the Seas, Emperor of India, and His Majesty the Emperor of All the Russias, animated by the sincere desire to settle by mutual agreement different questions concerning the interests of their States on the Continent of Asia, have determined to conclude Agreements destined to prevent all cause of misunderstanding between Great Britain and Russia in regard to the questions referred to, and have nominated for this purpose their respective Plenipotentiaries, to wit:

His Majesty the King of the United Kingdom of Great Britain and Ireland and of the British Dominions beyond the Seas, Emperor of India, the Right Honourable Sir Arthur Nicholson, His Majesty's Ambassador Extraordinary and Plenipotentiary to His Majesty the Emperor of All the Russias; the Master of his Court Alexander Iswolsky, Minister of Foreign Affairs;

Who, having communicated to each other their full powers, found in good and due form, have agreed on the following:-

ARRANGEMENT CONCERNING THIBET

The Governments of Great Britain and Russia recognising the suzerain rights of China in Thibet, and considering the fact that Great Britain, by reason of her geographical position, has a special interest in the maintenance of the status quo in the external relations of Thibet, have made the following arrangements:-

Article I

The two High Contracting Parties engage to respect the territorial integrity of Thibet and to abstain from all interference in the internal administration.

Article II

In conformity with the admitted principle of the suzerainty of China over Tibet, Great Britain and Russia engage not to enter into negotiations with Thibet except through the intermediary of the Chinese Government. This engagement does not exclude the direct relations between British Commercial Agents and the Thibetan authorities provided for in Article V of the Convention between Great Britain and Thibet of the 7th September 1904, and confirmed by the Convention between Great Britain and China of the 27th April 1906; nor does it modify the engagements entered into by Great Britain and China in Article I of the said Convention of 1906.

It is clearly understood that Buddhists, subjects of Great Britain or of Russia, may enter into direct relations on strictly religious matters with the Dalai Lama and the other representatives of Buddhism in Thibet; the Governments of Great Britain and Russia engage, as far as they are concerned, not to allow those relations to infringe the stipulations of the present arrangment.

Article III

The British and Russian Governments respectively engage not to send Representatives to Lhasa.

Article IV

The two High Contracting Parties engage neither to seek nor to obtain, whether for themselves or their subjects, any concessions for railways, roads, telegraphs, and mines, or other rights in Thibet.

Article V

The two Governments agree that no part of the revenues of Thibet, whether in kind or in cash, shall be pledged or assigned to Great Britain or Russia or to any of their subjects.

ANNEXE TO THE ARRANGEMENT BETWEEEN GREAT BRITAIN AND RUSSIA CONCERNING THIBET

Great Britain reaffirms the declaration, signed by His Excellency the Viceroy and Governor-General of India and appended to the Ratification of the Convention of the 7th September 1904, to the effect the occupation of the Chumbi Valley by British forces shall cease after the payment of three annual instalments of the indemnity of 25,00,000 rupees, provided that the trade marts mentioned in Article II of that Convention have been effectively opened for three years, and that in the meantime the Thibetan authorities have faithfully complied in all respects with the terms of the said Convention of 1904. It is clearly understood that if the occupation of the Chumbi Valley by the British forces has, for any reason, not been terminated at the time anticipated in the above Declaration, the British and Russian Governments will enter upon a friendly exchange of views on this subject.

The presence Convention shall be ratified, and the ratification exchanged at St. Petersburgh as soon as possible.

In witness whereof the respective Plenipotentiaries have signed the present Convention and affixed thereto their seals.

Done in duplicate at St. Petersburgh, the 18th (31st) August 1907.

Sd

ANNEXURE IX

Deed ceding Darjeeling to the English, 1 February 1835

TRANSLATION of the DEED of GRANT making over DARJEELING to the EAST INDIA COMPANY, dated 29th Maugh, Sumbut 1891, A.D., 1st February 1835.

The Governor-General having expressed his desire for the possession of the Hill of Darjeeling, on account of its cool climate, for the purpose of enabling the servants of his Government, suffering from sickness, to avail themselves of its advantages, I, the Sikkimputtee Rajah, out of friendship to the said Governor-General, hereby present Darjeeling to the East India Company, that is, all the land south of the Great Runjeet River, east of the Balasur, Kahail, and Little Runjeet Rivers, and west of the Rungno and Mahanuddi Rivers.

A. CAMPBELL,
Superintendent of Darjeeling,
and in charge of Political relations with Sikkim.

Seal of the Rajah prefixed to the document.

ANNEXURE X

No. _777_ /R.

Annexure X

From

C. A. Bell, Esquire, C. M. G.,
Political Officer in Sikkim.

To

His Highness the Maharaja of Sikkim,

G A N G T O K.

Dated Gangtok, the 29th March 1918.

Your Highness,

I have the honour to inform Your Highness that the Government of India have authorised me to make over to Your Highness the control of the following Departments of the Sikkim State, with effect from the 1st April 1918, namely:-

    (a) Excise

    (b) Income tax

    (c) Police

    (d) Jail and

    (e) Judicial and revenue Stamps.

                    I am,

             Your Highness's sincere friend,

                  Sd/- C. A. Bell.

                 Political Officer in Sikkim.

R. R. No. _246_

Date _29/3/16_ Memo No. _778_ /R.

File No.

Collection The Superintendent, Sikkim State, Gangtok.

Copy forwarded for information.

ANNEXURE XI

the 9th July, 1919.

My dear Maharaja Sahib,

        The Government of India have suggested
to Local Governments that the 19th July should be notified
as a public holiday, this being the date fixed for the
Peace Celebrations in England. As the hot weather is
unsuitable for celebrations in India the general
celebrations will take place in India next cold weather
but it is thought that the actual signing of the peace treaty
should not pass unnoticed in India. The public holiday
on the 19th July is therefore being arranged and I am
notifying it for my own offices and subordinate offices.
Flags will be flown and such other methods adopted as may
be suitable to indicate that the day is one of public
rejoicing. The Government of India have suggested to
Local Governments the advisability of arranging at all
principal centres throughout each province of all officials
and as many as possible of the non-official population
to whom the peace terms in connection with Germany would
be publicly summarized by the head of the district or other
chief local civil authority. I should like to arrange

that any non-officials who care to do so may be present
at the meeting which I propose to hold for Government
servants on the 19th July as the Government of India think
it desirable that the nature of the peace terms imposed on
Germany should be made known as widely as possible.

The weather makes it unlikely that an outdoor
meeting can be arranged and so I propose to hold the
meeting in one of the vacant barracks as being perhaps
the largest room available.   I shall be grateful for
Your Highness's co-operation in letting the general public
know that the meeting is open to all and hope to have an
opportunity of discussing details at an early date.

I remain,

Yours very sincerely

His Highness
    Maharaja Tashi Namgyal, C.I.E.,
        Maharaja of Sikkim,
            The Palace,
                Gangtok.

ANNEXURE XII

SIKKIM STATE.

GENERAL DEPARTMENT.
* * * * * *

No. 919 /G.B.,

From

    The SECRETARY to

      HIS HIGHNESS the MAHARAJA of SIKKIM.

To

    Barmiak Lama.

      G a n g t o k.

Dated Gangtok, Sikkim, the 3rd July, 1919.

     In view of the signing of the Peace Treaty between the Allies and Germany, His Highness the Maharaja has ordered that special Peace prayers in all the monasteries in Sikkim should be repeated for three days that the coming years of Peace may ever be happy and prosperous.

                 Secretary to
          His Highness the Maharaja of Sikkim.

ANNEXURE XIII

To

    His Highness Maharaja Tashi Namgyal, C.I.E.,
        Maharaja of Sikkim.

My Esteemed Friend,

    Your Highness has no doubt seen the Royal Proclamation of His Majesty the King Emperor dated the 16th August, 1920, which concludes with the following gracious words :

    "Although it has not pleased Providence that OUR DEAR SON should carry OUR GREETINGS on this occasion, We shall send in his stead OUR UNCLE, HIS ROYAL HIGHNESS FIELD MARSHAL THE DUKE OF CONNAUGHT to inaugurate on OUR behalf the Chamber of Princes ...., to take part in other ceremonies which he would have performed, and to convey to the Princes and peoples of India the messages which it had been OUR hope to entrust to him".

    In accordance with the message of His Majesty the King Emperor I invite Your Highness to be present at Delhi on the occasion of the ceremony of the inauguration of the Chamber of Princes to be held at the Diwan-i-Am on the 8th of February 1921.

          I remain, with much consideration,
            Your Highness' sincere friend,

                Viceroy and Governor-General of India.

Delhi :
The 22 November 1920.

230

ANNEXURE XIV

" The Palace "

Gangtok, Sikkim.

The 9th October, 1920.

My Friend,

      I send you, for your information, a post copy of my telegram of today's date respecting my going to Delhi to attend the inauguration ceremony of the "Chamber "of Princes".

      I shall write more fully, if need be, later. I am confined to my room, but am very glad to say that at last there is marked improvement. Thanks to kindly aid from local helpers.

                    Yours very sincerely,

                    Maharaja of Sikkim.

To,

      C. A. Bell, Esquire., C.M.G., C.I.E.,

           Political Officer in Sikkim.

ANNEXURE XV

VICEREGAL LODGE,
SIMLA.

9th May 1919.

My Friend,

I greatly regret to inform Your Highness that the Amir Amanulla has, without warning and without provocation, moved troops to the Indian frontier and has committed acts of hostility which render inevitable a collision between our forces and those of Afghanistan.

I enclose for Your Highness' information a copy of the official announcement which has been issued on the subject. From this it will be seen that after the assassination of the late Amir Habibulla, his third son Amanulla Khan seized the throne, and with the enforced approval of an assembly of elders and notables, specially convened for the purpose, condemned to death Colonel Ali Reza, the supposed murderer, and imprisoned for life Sardar Nasrulla Khan, the brother of the late Ruler. The suspicion soon grew, however, that the real assassins had escaped and that innocent persons had been made to suffer in their stead. The occupants of high offices, and even Amanulla himself, were suspected of complicity in the crime, and discontent and disaffection appear to have spread rapidly through the State. As Amanulla's position became more and more insecure, he evidently resolved, like many another Ruler in similar case, to lead his people into war in order to divert their thoughts from internal affairs, and in the hope that victory might unite them in allegiance to him.

In making this wanton and audacious attack upon India, the Amir is guilty of the basest ingratitude because, as the world knows, the Government of India have given constant and generous proofs of their friendship towards his country. Amanulla's insensate policy contrasts deplorably with the wisdom and statesmanship which characterised Habibulla's reign, and it will sooner or later be condemned by all sober and right-minded people in the State.

We are fully prepared to meet the attack, since we possess overwhelming superiority in the materials of war, such as artillery, machine guns, aeroplanes and transport, while our troops are numerous and well trained and ample reserves are at our disposal from the recent theatres of war, should they be required. We therefore have every hope that, if the conflict must occur, victory will be speedy.

To the many Muslims, both in British India and the States, the outbreak of war with a neighbouring Muslim power must necessarily be a matter of distress. They will learn however from the terms of the public announcement that the quarrel was unsought and unprovoked by us, and I am convinced that, true to their splendid traditions, they will remain firm in their devotion to the British Government, which has brought peace and prosperity to them and to the other peoples of India.

I need hardly ask that Your Highness will do all that lies in your power to guide and encourage your Muslim subjects at this moment.

Further, we must anticipate that, both in British India and in the States, a war on the frontier may swell the forces of disorder, since to ill-balanced minds it will appear to afford an opportunity for rejecting restraints which are imposed in the interests of order and good government. For this reason it is necessary to watch closely the activities of persons who may be bent on creating excitement and trouble, and to be prepared with measures for the prevention or suppression of any agitation or disturbance that may manifest itself.

In all these matters I feel assured that I can place full reliance, as in the past, on Your Highness' utmost support and co-operation during the period of stress which may lie before us.

I remain,

Your Highness' sincere friend,

Viceroy and Governor-General of India.

To

His Highness Maharaja Tashi Namgyal, C.I.E.,

Maharaja of Sikkim.

ANNEXURE XVI

THE PALACE,
Gangtok,
The 18th May 1919.

My friend,

I beg to acknowledge the receipt of Your Excellency's favour of the 9th May 1919 and to express my surprise at hearing of the audacity shown in the unprovoked act of hostility on the part of the Amir of Afghanistan.

I however feel quite sure that he will soon be brought to his senses and compelled to see the folly of the step he has presumed to take against the India Government.

I beg to assure Your Excellency of the firm faith and loyalty of my little State and of my own sincere allegiance to the King Emperor and my readiness to do my best.

The number of Muslim subjects in my little State is so small that I am sure to be able to prevent them from creating any trouble.

I Subscribe myself,
Your Excellency's Sincere friend

T. Namgal

MAHARAJA of SIKKIM.

ANNEXURE XVII

Indo-Sikkim Treaty of 1950

The president of India and His Highness the Maharaja of Sikkim being desirous of further strengthening the good relations already existing between India and Sikkim have resolved to enter into a new treaty with each other and the President of India has for the purpose appointed as his plenipotentiary Shri Harishwar Dayal, Political Officer in Sikkim and His Highness the Maharaja having examined Hariswar Dayal's credentials and found them good and in due form the two have agreed as follows:

Article I

All previous treaties between the British Government and Sikkim, which are at present in force as between India and Sikkim, are hereby formally cancelled.

Article II

Sikkim shall continue to be a protectorate of India and subject to the provisions of this, Treaty shall enjoy autonomy m regards to Its Internal affairs.

Article III

1. The Government of India will be responsible for the defense and territorial integrity of Sikkim. It shall have the right to take such measures as it considers necessary for the defense of Sikkim and security of India, whether preparatory or otherwise, and whether within or outside Sikkim. In particular, the Government of India shall have the right to station troops anywhere within Sikkim.

2. The measures referred to in Para 1 will as far as possible be taken by the Government of India in consultation with the Government of Sikkim.

3. The Government of Sikkim shall not import any arms ammunitions, military sores or stores other warlike materials of any description for any purpose whatsoever without the previous consent of the Government of India.

Article IV

1. The external relations of Sikkim whether political, economical or financial shall be conducted and regulated solely by the Government of India and the Government of Sikkim shall have no dealings with any foreign power.

2. Subjects of Sikkim traveling to foreign countries shall be treated as Indian protected for the purpose of passports and shall receive from Indian representatives abroad the same protections and facilities as Indian nationals.

Article 1V

The Government of Sikkim agrees not to levy any import duty, transit duty or other imports on the goods brought into, or in transit through Sikkim, and the Government of India agrees not to levy any import or other duty on goods of sikkimese origin brought into India from Sikkim.

Article VI

1. The Government of India shall have the exclusive right of constructing, maintaining and regulating the use of railways, aerodromes and landing grounds and air navigation facilities, posts, telegraphs, telephones and wireless installations in Sikkim and the Government of Sikkim shall render the Government of India every assistance in their constructions, maintenance and protection.

2. The Government of Sikkim may, however, construct maintain and: regulate the use of railways and aerodromes and landing grounds and air navigation facilities to such extent as may be agreed to by the Government of India.

3. The Government of India shall have the right to construct and maintain in Sikkim the roads for strategic purposes and for the purpose of improving communications with India and other adjoining countries; and the Government of Sikkim shall render the Government of India every assistance in the construction, maintenance and protection of such roads.

Article VII

1. Subjects of Sikkim shall have the right of entry into and free movement within India, and Indian nationals shall have the right of entry into and free movement within Sikkim.

2. 'Subject to such regulations as the Government of Sikkim may prescribe in consultation with the Government of India, Indian nationals shall have:

    (a) The right to carry on trade and commerce in Sikkim; and

    (b) When established in any trade in Sikkim, the right to acquire, hold and dispose of any property, movable or immovable, for the purposes of their trade or residence in Sikkim.

3. Subjects of Sikkim shall have the same right;

    (i) To carry on trade and commerce in India, and to employment therein; and

    (ii) Of acquiring, holding and disposing of property, movable and immovable as Indian nationals.

Article VIII

1. Indian nationals within Sikkim shall be subject to the laws of Sikkim and subjects of Sikkim within India shall be subject to the laws of India.

2. Whenever any criminal proceedings are initiated in Sikkim against any Indian national or any person in the service of Government of India or any foreigner, the Government of Sikkim shall furnish the Representative of the Government of India in Sikkim (hereinafter referred to as the Indian Representative) with particulars of the charges against such person.

In the case of any person in the service of the Government of India or any foreigner it is so demanded by the Indian Representative, such person shall be handed over to him for trial before such courts as may be established for the purpose by the Government of India either in Sikkim or outside.

Article IX

1. The Government of Sikkim agree to seize and deliver up any fugitive offender from outside Sikkim who has taken refuge therein on demand being made by the Indian Representative. Should any delay occur in complying with such demand, the Indian Police may follow the person whose surrender has been demanded into any part of Sikkim, and shall on showing a warrant signed by the Indian Representative, receive every assistance and protection in the prosecution of their object from the Sikkim Officers.

2. The Government of India similarly agrees, on demand being made by the Government of Sikkim, to take extradition proceeding against and surrender, any fugitive offender from Sikkim who has taken refuge in the territory of India.

3. In this article, "fugitive offender" means a person who is accused of having committed an extradition offence as defined in the First Schedule b the Indian Extradition act 1903 or any other offence which may hereafter be agreed upon between the Government of India and the Government of Sikkim as being an extradition offence.

Article X

The Government of India, having in mind the friendly relations already existing between India and Sikkim and now further strengthened by this Treaty, and being desirous of assisting in the development and good administration of Sikkim, agrees to pay the Government of Sikkim a sum of rupees three lakhs every year so long as the terms of this Treaty are duly observed by the Government of Sikkim. The first payment under this article will be made before the end of the year 1950 and subsequent payments will be made in the month of August every year.

Article XI

The Government of India shall have the right to appoint a representative to reside in Sikkim; and the Government of Sikkim shall provide him and his staff with all reasonable facilities in regard to their carrying out their duties in Sikkim.

Article XII

If any dispute arises in the interpretation of the provisions of this Treaty which cannot be resolved by mutual consultation, the dispute shall be referred to the Chief Justice of India whose decision therein shall be final.

Article XIII

This Treaty shall come into force without ratification from the date of signature by both the parties.

Done in duplicate at Gangtok on this 5th day of December 1950..

<table>
<tr><td>**(Sd)**</td><td>**(Sd)**</td></tr>
<tr><td>**HARISHWARDAYAL**</td><td>**TASHNAMGYAL**</td></tr>
<tr><td>**Political Officer**</td><td>**His Highness the**</td></tr>
<tr><td>**in Sikkim**</td><td>**Maharaja of Sikkim**</td></tr>
</table>